Praise for *WARPATH*

"How do you live and raise a family when the location of your chosen home is on an Indian warpath? Hostile Indians and warring European nations pose an ever present threat to your very life.

Historians marvel at the interconnection between the lives of the Martin family and the frontier events that led to the founding of America.

Little did John Martin realize how the selection of Southwest Pennsylvania would place his wife and children in harm's way. This is a true story of a frontier family.

Attacked by savages, kidnapped and separated across hundreds of miles of frontier, would the love for one another and the desire to live sustain his family during the years of painful separation and strife?

Explore the lives of the Martin family and add them to the list of early American heroes along with Gist's, Boone's, Washington's, Stobo's . . . .

Rock Foster, Author of:
When Gauley Ran Blood* and *On Banks of Gauley

This story is a novel but it is based on solid facts, most of which came from the Pennsylvania Archives, and such interesting sources as Fred Anderson's *Crucible of War* and C. Hale Sipe's *Indian Wars of Pennsylvania*. Sipes plowed through an unindexed set of Archives and published in 1932. The authors were privileged to hear Fred Anderson lecture at U. of Pittsburgh's Greensburg Campus. Anderson's novel idea is that the French and Indian War (Seven Years War) should really be called World War I since it was fought not only in Europe and North America but also in Calcutta and the Caribbean. The French and British and their various allies had battled for European dominance but the venue had enlarged to the fight for world dominance.

The events, places, and people were real. Some of the actual conversations were in the Archives. Where there were not actual conversations, we filled in some, making this a novel. The colonists observed the British army up close and decided that they could beat them when push came to shove. When the Parliament tried to recoup the monies used in the war, by taxing everything from documents to tea, the colonists resentment turned from the French and Indians to the British and the King.

Pennsylvania was ready for the American Revolution.

WARPATH

A Saga of the Frontier Family of John Martin

*For Shannon,
Enjoy the history!
Charles R. Martin
Sally Martin*

Charles R. Martin
& Sara Mitchell Martin

Copyright © 2008 by Charles R. Martin & Sara Mitchell Martin.

Library of Congress Control Number: 2008905813
ISBN: Hardcover   978-1-4363-5315-1
               Softcover   978-1-4363-5314-4

All rights reserved. No part of this book may be reproduced or transmitted in any form or by any means, electronic or mechanical, including photocopying, recording, or by any information storage and retrieval system, without permission in writing from the copyright owner.

This book was printed in the United States of America.

To order additional copies of this book, contact:
Xlibris Corporation
1-888-795-4274
www.Xlibris.com
Orders@Xlibris.com

Chapter I

Fulton County, Pennsylvania

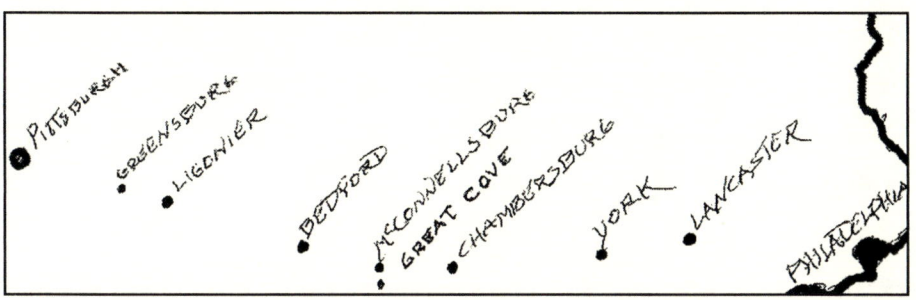

The path was barely visible. It was not much more than pieces of clay that had been trampled into a hard, bare spot, between the rock rubble, not more than a foot wide zigzagging over the Tuscarawas Ridge in the area known to the few frontier travelers as "Stony Batter." The hoof clattering of the struggling horses and the sweating men who were ahead up the path made John slow down and talk to his sweet Nellie. Nellie was not happy to be going up the rocky trail but John's patience soothed her anxiety. She snorted and nuzzled his jacket looking for a treat. He groped through his pockets and found a last dried apple for the sorrel horse. James, the first struggling fellow ahead, grunted as he all but pushed his balky mule up the last, steeper height suddenly shouted:

"Oh, look! I can see the valley! It is beautiful!"

The horse behind John looked up expectantly as it felt the fatigue begin to fall away from the humans. John urged Nellie and they crested the path and looked down at the valley spread out before them and made room for the horses and men who followed. The pile of rubble rock and house sized boulders that gave them a view through the thick forest, was spread wide enough for them to group together to gape at their destination. The valley was long but not too wide and, of course, covered with trees. First there was the zigzag of the hard won primitive trail, then the overwhelming, oppressive, forest. There seemed to be a stream meandering north/south through the middle, and another towering mountain range beyond. James studied his carefully drawn map and said, "This has to be it. This is the Great Cove!"

The four men collected at the gap took off their hats and paused for prayer, led by John. He knew they expected something special from his offering but felt Nellie's need to get to the creek for a drink also and kept it to a short prayer of thanks for having reached their "promised land." Two of the other horses started down and skidded on their haunches for the first twenty feet, scattering tools and making the men cuss a bit and then end up laughing at having cussed right after a prayer. John eased Nellie down and waited for the others to reassemble after collecting shovels, axes, awls, saws and the other things that they had been assured they would need. An hour later they were at the creek. It was not wide enough to present a problem crossing. They turned south and where a small stream came in from the East, John said,

"James, isn't this my spot? See that creek there? I think this is my spot. I'll stop here and scout around."

"It looks like it to me, too. I just hope this map is good. Further down south there where the mountain ranges meet, should be Webster's land. Mine must be beyond this range, in the Licking Creek valley," said James. They looked at the German and he nodded and smiled.

"Goot."

The German responded, "Goot, ya. Goot."

"Who gets Abraham?" asked Will Webster, "With his carpentry skills, he will be a great help."

"His cow would be nice for Captain Stewart, and I think Stewart said that he had a bit of pasture," said James.

The cow had seized the opportunity stop to munch on the native grass growing by the creek. While they watched her, she walked into the creek, up to her belly, and lifting her chin gave a long, loud moo of contentment.

"Shh. Shh," said Abraham. The short, stocky German put his hand behind his ear to indicate listening. The rest listened and heard an echoing moo from a distance.

"Goot. Bool," Said Abraham, obviously delighted with the opportunity for bovine nuptials in the near future.

"We need a plan to meet again," said John. "We need to locate Captain Stewart's place and meet there. We promised to help him build. He has a wife and I'll bet she is making his life miserable if he doesn't have her cabin built yet."

They laughed again, and agreed to meet again on the next Sunday at Stewart's place, which, according to the map, should be just south of John's land.

"Wait a minute," said Will Webster, "We don't really know where Captain Stewart's place is!"

"I was just thinking that wisp of smoke we saw coming from down the creek might be his. If it is, good. If it isn't, it will be our new neighbor and he might know where Captain Stewart is. You can look into it on your way down stream."

John sat down on a rock to think and watch his companions disappear into the forest. His first concern was always for

Nellie. There was precious little grass in the forest but the area around the creek was more open and swampy and short native grasses were growing there, more than the cow had been able to gobble up. He hobbled Nellie, unloaded the tools and supplies that she had been carrying and let her graze while he scouted. Up the small hill to the west he found a rocky outcropping and sunlight enough to have another grassy glade. Another hour's search turned up an open field, an amazing thing here in the forest. It looked as if a human hand had worked here. Brush was beginning to grow but it was at least two acres of sunlight in the forest, with the small stream nearby. He thought he could put his cabin right in the middle of the clearing where strangers could be seen approaching and the sun would warm it.

Back at the creek, sitting on a rock that was a perfect seat for fishing in the small pool, John brought out his precious fish hook and loaded it with a live grass hopper. He soon had a couple of small fish for his dinner. He made a fire to cook it and worked on preparing a lean-to to sleep under.

He was crouched in front of the fire when he realized that someone was there. When he lifted his eyes, standing, not three feet from him, was a young Indian brave. The Indian was calm and relaxed. His arms were folded over his chest. John quieted his anxiety and stood up and found himself to be almost a head taller than the dark skinned man. The Indian lifted his right hand in greeting and John, who had folded his arms as the Indian had done, lifted his in return. The Indian made a gesture that John understood to mean smoking. He dug into his pocket and came up with his precious pouch of tobacco. The Indian nodded and smiled and sat down. John sat down on the ground also and got out his beloved clay pipe. Pipes were fragile and often broke. This one was still good. John carefully packed the bowl with tobacco and took a couple of deep puffs to get it started. He passed it to the Indian who took a couple of puffs also. He pointed to himself and said his name, "John Martin." The Indian passed the pipe back and did the same. His name was Shingas.

John reached his right hand to Shingas and they shook, white man style.

"Shingas land," said the Indian, "Indian land."

John felt a great cloud of anxiety descending over him. It could be that this was, indeed, Indian land.

Not knowing what to answer, he nodded and smiled.

"You buy Indian land?" The Indian did not smile back.

"Yes. I bought land from white man."

"My land."

John was staggered. It could very well be that the Washington from whom he had bought his parcel had no right to sell the land! His jaw dropped. The Indian offered the pipe back and John just stared at him so Shingas took another puff.

"You buy land from Shingas."

John could not think of what he could use to buy the land this second time. He had invested every last penny in the gear that he was carrying. He shook his head and shrugged his shoulders.

"I have no more money."

"Give Shingas horse."

John could not imagine life without Nellie who was his pet as well as his servant. How alone he would be. His head sunk into his hands. He got up and found another couple of branches to put in the fire. Shingas had finished the pipe and was picking up the tobacco pouch and stuffing it and the pipe into his shirt.

"Horse, me. Land, you." Shingas got up and walked down to the creek where Nellie was munching on grass. He took off her hobble and grabbed her bridle and walked away with her.

John watched them disappear into the dark. It had been a long day, he rolled up in his blanket and went to sleep after first asking for the patience to understand his new neighbor.

* * *

The next morning, John had another visitor. This one was a totally imposing, impressive Irishman. If you were called Irish in a place where Scotch-Irish were in large numbers, you were probably Catholic and would be viewed with great suspicion by the Scotch-Irish Presbyterians. George Croghan, actually an Episcopalian, was huge by anyone's standard. He owned the largest frontier store, had the largest trading business with the Indians, and had the most influence in Philadelphia of any frontiersman. He showed up as John was finishing a breakfast of corn meal cooked in a skillet. He was happy to finish up the leftovers that John had planned to use for lunch. He was amiable and full of stories about the Indians with whom he could communicate very well, and Quakers with whom he could communicate enough.

"You should not be here. This is Indian land."

This was obviously the message that he had come to deliver. John did not know how to respond so he listened while Croghan went on to explain at great length that the payment John had given Washington and the Ohio Company meant nothing here because this was not Virginia, or even Maryland, it was Pennsylvania.

"In Pennsylvania, we pay the Indians for the land before we steal it from them. No one has paid for this land. I am in negotiations with the Delaware Indians now. The Delaware are Shingas and King Beaver, actually the Lenai Lenape. Most of them have already left this area and have moved to the valley of the Beautiful River, but they have not yet sold it. I am negotiating with them. And when they come to terms, and sell, I have an option on this land and will be selling it. At that time, you can buy it from me."

"So I didn't have to pay Shingas?"

"If I were you, I would do what ever it takes to keep Shingas happy. He is a prince and his father, or perhaps it is his brother, is King Beaver of the Lenai Lenape tribe. Their history is complicated. They were beaten in battle by the Six Nations a while back. They are, therefore, subservient to the Six Nations who consider them 'women'. The Six Nations negotiated with Penn and sold the Delaware land, and took the money and gifts and gave nothing to the Lenai Lenape who had to move out the very wonderful Delaware Valley. You may have noticed as you traveled through that it is the richest land anyone ever farmed. Now the Iroquois have told them to move on beyond the mountains to the Ohio River Valley and they have pretty much left here. Actually, of course, I am negotiating with the Iroquois for the land."

"So does it keep on going that the Lenai Lenape will have their land sold again and they get nothing but a move out notice?" asked John.

Croghan nodded.

John added, "So let me get this right: I bought this land from the Ohio Company. The Pennsylvanians tell me it wasn't the Ohio

Company's land to sell and that the land belongs to the Indians. Then Shingas comes along, we eat together and smoke a pipe together, and he says that this is Indian land and takes my horse Nellie away in exchange for the land. Now you, Croghan, tell me that you are going to buy this land and you will sell it to me. Tell me, Croghan, how many times do I have to buy this land? I'm beginning to think that I am back in Ireland where you have to be a pal of the king to get land. I have more sympathy with Shingas than anyone. Neither of us can claim this same land."

"Well, I can't either, yet. And that is about the size of it. In the meantime, it is very dangerous to be here. We don't know if or when the Lenai Lenape will run out of patience with the Six Nations or the English and go on the warpath. They have been very peaceful up until now but that is partly because of the way they revered William Penn, the Quaker. Penn's sons are nothing like that noble man. They are bloodsuckers if there ever were ones, even if they are Quakers. I am a buffer between them and the Indians. I give lavish gifts out of my own pocket to the chiefs to keep them happy. You may end up doing that, too. It is the cheapest, safest way to keep the peace. By the way, Shingas passed me on the trail this morning. He had a new horse with him. He told me about you and your friends. He seems pretty calm now but you never know. These savages all train to be warriors. Killing is what they do, normally, but the Lenai Lenape have been held down for a long time. The other tribes forbid them their natural instinct in the killing thing and so they are sometimes proud of keeping the peace with William Penn. It is not easy to understand."

Croghan paused and then looked skyward and shook his head and sighed.

"The tribes have all lost members to war and disease. I heard that there are no more than about one hundred thousand of them in the North East and only about three or four thousand of them are warriors. They capture people for slaves and make some captives members of the tribe to fill in for those who have died. I have known full grown white men who have spent most of their lives as Indians and can't even speak English any more."

"Then there are the stinking French," Croghan continued. "They are trying to stir our Indians up against us and are building forts on land that we English have claimed. The French give gifts also. The one good thing is that the English items that I sell are a lot better and less expensive than the goods the French sell. There are about twenty English to every Frenchman on this new world, so we should be able to handle those rotters. By the way, is there anything you might need? I have a full warehouse."

"I am totally broke, I have no way to pay."

"I can always use extra help at Aughwick. It is only over that next hill and a bit north and great supply of store goods. I will probably move there. Right now I live on this side of the Susquehanna." Croghan sat up and looked behind John. John heard a familiar noise and did not turn around to look. It was the sound of a horse's fairly rapid approach. His Nellie ran up and bumped him from behind. John laughed and rubbed her nose as she stuck it over his shoulder.

Croghan said, "She has company."

John jumped up and saw that Nellie had brought a friend, a young and very enthusiastic stallion. He was too skittish to come up to the two men. He stood at the edge of the clearing, stomping his feet and whinnying at Nellie.

"That stallion looks just like one of mine," said Croghan. He tried to approach the horse for a closer look. The horse ducked his head and seemed to bare his teeth.

Croghan gave up with a shake of his head.

"He's a wild one. I never found anyone who could deal with him. Last time I saw him Shingas was leading your horse, and that stallion was free and moseying behind, shaking his head up and down and snorting. I'd like to think that he gave Shingas problems, too. I could send some of my boys back to catch him but the chances of them catching him are not good and if they did, he is just a lot of trouble."

Croghan and John were both laughing at the affection that Nellie was showing John.

"Looks like your horse didn't want to be an Indian and they got together. I don't know what your Indian friend will think of this. He's liable to be back, but may be not. He might think he was losing face because your Nellie decided to go home. Either way, be careful. You're just never really sure with the Indians," Croghan was still laughing.

"Well, I must be going. Will you tell your friends here about the Indians and about Aughwick? Thanks for breakfast. Remember, I will be glad to sell you this very land after I get title to it."

As the big fellow about to disappear into the forest, he turned and yelled back at John, "If you can tame this horse he is yours."

John scratched his head and smiled. He noticed a little rodent with its tail straight up over its back, dash onto his cooled cooking pan, stuff the last crumb of his breakfast into its cheeks and sprint off into the woods.

"I sure get some interesting guests," he said to Nellie, rubbing her ears. The stallion had started to graze and drink from the creek. He gave every indication of staying.

A huge black bird that had been walking carefully around the fire area made a peck at a shinny thing and before John could react, had snatched and, with a great fuss had flown away with: his only fishing hook.

Chapter II

Making a Home on the Frontier

By 1735, 25 year old John Martin had a primitive log cabin on the land that he claimed as his land, and it had some big problems. However he was very amiable and did not worry about a few leaks in the roof or visits from the nearby forest creatures. He had come from a well-settled and actually, comparatively comfortable life in Ireland. It was amazing, even to him, that he and his friends had just kept moving west, and a bit north, past the handsome homes in the city of Philadelphia, past the beautiful farms of the Germans, past the small, rough frontier village of Chambers Mill. He was glad that he was not alone, and that his friends shared his passion for religion.

Other land—starved Scotch-Irish had come from his Irish county of Antrim. The large families, the poverty, and the lack of land had made the grim future of Ireland seem like a black cloud hanging over the community. Families would take up collections to buy their youngest sons a chance in the far off land of milk and honey that they felt their Bibles had promised them. The friends that John made on the ship that brought them over were also devout Presbyterians. They believed that their prayers had saved them from the terrible attacks of small pox that had killed almost every third person on that ship during the terrible trip. They, being Presbyterians, believed that God had chosen them for great things. They crowded together to read John's Bible.

John had done his best to share the expensive education that he had been blessed with by teaching his companions to read and work sums. His new friend James Mitchell had an uncle whose family were surveyors and had sent James money to come to Pennsylvania to help with surveying. Through this friend's contacts, John heard about the land beyond the mountains. He worked for the surveyor and then for the German farmers in Northampton long enough to earn enough money to put a payment down on the piece of land beyond the mountains, beyond Chambersburg. He and James had made the big effort to keep in touch and now were neighbors.

John had quit the job with the surveyor to work for the German farmers. He liked their hearty meals, solid, warm homes and barns full of hay and grain. He learned everything he knew about farming in this new land from the Germans. He developed a strong love for the great horses who worked so willingly in the rich fields. The Germans always seemed to be three steps ahead of the Scotch-Irish. Their farming skills were better because they had been well-to-do farmers in Germany. They were all either Lutheran or Reformed Church and held together tightly to build the beautiful barns and houses for the members of their communities. John realized that there was much to be learned from these solid people. They, on the other hand liked John because he was a very good worker, industrious from dawn until dark. They would kid him saying that one day he might be a good farmer. He picked up basic German quickly and his sunny disposition and gentle joking made him always welcome at their evening firesides. He could not share their plentiful beer because his family believed that the Scotch-Irish had a weakness where alcohol was concerned. His family felt that many a good man had gone down to misery and shame because of alcohol and it was better not to give the Satan in "Demon Rum" an opening. However, John did give in to the fragrant odor of the burning tobacco that swirled around from the German farmers' pipes and bought a long clay pipe so he could join the Germans in smoking. The pipe that Shingas had confiscated was but one of what would be many gifts to the young Indian prince.

The Germans had had to swear allegiance to England when they got off the boat in the colony so they were also happy to learn some English from John Martin. For them, the gracious farmland of Pennsylvania was plain and barren compared to the cities, cathedrals, and castles of the Palatinate and they had some homesick spells. They tried to cure their bouts of longing for home by telling tales of how the 500,000 of the Palatinate had been reduced to a tenth of that during the plagues and by European wars that leveled cities and never seemed to stop. They wanted peace to reign forever in the new land. In the old country, they could be conscripted into an army and marched off to fight wars that they did not understand or care about. The only fight that they would have willingly engaged in would have been against the awful Mohammedan Turks and those dreadful enemies had been left far behind.

John had found peace at the cleared land in Great Cove. The Indians who had been there before John had cleared a couple of acres by girdling the trees. The trees had died, leaving a bit of sunshine in the dark forest. They would plant their corn, using a pointed stick, and put a fish in the hole to fertilize the hungry corn plant. After a time, years, the tree would come down and rot away and the patient Indian would have a field. But, then, the Indians had left the field in Great Cove and John was happy to move in and claim it as his own.

He decided not to worry about the title to the land that he felt he had bought from a Virginia company, the "Ohio Company." Later, Quakers told him that William Penn and Lord Calvert, the Papist, had been in dispute about the boundary between Pennsylvania and Maryland. They asserted that there was no way that Virginia could claim the Cumberland Valley or Cove valley. Impossible. However, he should not be in the valley beyond the first mountain range because that was Indian land.

John's agreement with the Virginia Company was that he was to have cleared the land and lived on it to maintain his agreement with the Virginia Colony. He tried to get the Quakers to go along with his owning the land but they insisted that he should not be there. He decided that since there wasn't much he could do, that he just would not worry.

John was tall and fair haired and blue eyed. His arms and back were strong from the heavy work of clearing the land. Nellie, the sorrel horse had come back that time when Shingas took her as payment for Indian land. Much to John's amusement, she was accompanied by a handsome and enthusiastic stallion. That meant that John had to build a stout corral to keep Nellie from just leaving with the other horse. This, before he could work on his own housing. He found a grove of locust and used the gnarled wood for posts, as the Germans had taught him. Nellie seemed sad when the stallion departed but later, she was joined by colts that kept her company. Nellie was a good horse, pleasant and willing but just not up to a lot of the heavy work. Clearing the land to build the cabin and grow food for Nellie and her colts had taken most of John's time and effort. John always had big plans and for these plans, he needed money. Cash was not easy to come by on the frontier so he trapped the smaller fur animals and hunted the larger ones.

He worked out a system with some nearby Lenai Lenape Indians who had not yet left the area. He would track down and shoot a deer with his heavy musket and then carry some of the meat and the skin to the Indian camp. He had learned a few words in Indian and would wave his arms around a bit and the squaw would exchange cured skins for the fresh ones and some dried meat for the fresh meat. Sometimes he was able to get some fresh or smoked fish from them. It was a pleasant time for everyone and he would have a bit to eat and smoke with the braves and carry the furs back to his cabin.

It was fall and John needed to go to the city to exchange the furs for winter supplies. This year, he had an especially good pile of furs to exchange. And, he had the really good idea. As he loaded the pelts on the wagon and hitched Nellie up he was thinking some more about his idea and whistling cheerfully and started off enthusiastically.

The path up to the Mitchell place didn't look much used and he worried about that a bit. Some of the settlers had become discouraged and gone back to the towns. James had not showed up for a couple of Sundays. He stopped at the Stewart place to chat a bit and get news. The news was hardly ever good.

"So how is the Stewart Family doing? Is the Captain around?"

"No, John just left this morning to go to York to pick up some supplies. He's thinking of building something strong, like a small fort. We just might need something like that one of these days."

She pushed on the big pile of dough in the dough trough. "I made some corn bread this morning, would you like some?"

"I love corn bread. Thanks. Now, about that fort. I was talking to Abraham Leasure and James Mitchell about that very thing. I'm sure we can all help and put up a fort in a hurry. It would be best near your family; you have so many children already. The rest of us bachelors would be handy in case of trouble. Tell John to see me when he gets back and we will plan where to put it and how to build it."

"I'm glad you are so ready to help. Thank you for that." Mary sliced off a nice piece of corn bread and John stuffed a big bite in his mouth and waved goodbye. He paused long enough to wish her joy at the impending birth of the fifth Stewart child and to say that he would be gone for six weeks to make some money working the harvest for the Germans at York.

He retraced his steps and then headed east up and over the Stony Batter and down to Chambers Mill. Three days after that busy village, he came into York. In this area were many Germans who still spoke German and always seem pretty gruff when John came in with pelts. He went down the carefully paved streets through the handsome, simple, stone houses to three different traders and found that he would have a very good year. Pelts had been scarce and the price was high. When the deals were completed he was delighted. He drove his wagon north to Northampton to a German farm where he had made acquaintances earlier. There, the buildings were, as in York, built of the limestone that is such a trial to the plow. The barn was massive and ornamented with trim that had been carefully crafted. The rich fields were edged with walls of the stone that is both a welcome and unwelcome crop as it comes popping up to the surface.

John was as adept at letting the Germans know that he wanted to work as he was in trading with the Indians.

After working several days he got the German farmer to understand that what he wanted for his help with the harvesting work would be a pair of the great horses that were being bred on the farm. The mighty Percherons were even gentler than John remembered. They worked tirelessly pulling big plows through the fertile soil.

The Germans were planting winter wheat as soon as they harvested the big ears of corn. John was put to work with a scythe and demonstrated his ability to learn and adapt and work harder than even the young German men. His dedication and good humor made him a popular person and he was soon treated like a member of the family. The buxom girls would bring him special treats and flirt, but John was interested in the one other English-speaking person, the Red-haired milk-maid. Her name was Margery and she was adept at milking the cow, churning butter, and making cheese. Everyone worked very hard to prepare for the winter.

Of the many young mares, John timidly chose the smallest. He could see that it would be harder to feed them than his small horse and he was afraid that he did not have enough oats or hay stored for the winter to keep both his horse and the pair of the great horses but he might get by with a pregnant mare and his horse, Nellie.

By November, most of the harvest was in and John knew that the family would not need his help much longer. After much dickering, he settled for a young, impregnated, mare. She was sizeable, heavy of bone, sweet tempered, and with a deep chest, and the most beautiful horse that John had ever known. She was four years old and could produce young for at least another fifteen years. She was already named Berthe by the German family.

The longer nights also brought more free time.

John's ideas began to turn to just how lonely it would be when he returned to the mountain valley and complete isolation when the snows came. He was more and more attracted to tall, strong, big-boned Margery, who was just 2 years younger than he was. She was so good to talk to, humorous and knew about things like politics.

She was an avid reader. She liked to read the popular Philadelphia paper published by the amusing and philosophical Benjamin Franklin. She was knowledgeable about things going on in the colonies. John had learned to read by reading the Bible. His ability to remember long passages from the Psalms and the New Testament gave him standing in the Scotch-Irish community. The flowing poetry of the King James Version was a source of beauty and charm for him. His devotion to his religion fascinated Margery and she loved spending time with him.

Finally, the German family, rather than feed him over the winter, told him that it was time to leave. They did it nicely, imploring him to come back next year. Margery was in tears. John had made her promise to wait for him to come for her in the spring when she would have worked off her indenture and be free to leave the family who had paid for her passage from England.

John had not ever thought that he would not be happy to be returning to the Great Cove and he was happy, but sad and lonely, too. He had filled his wagon with food supplies and oats for the horses and trade items for the Indians. When he arrived at his cabin he was pleased to see that he would be able to do more haying, and set to work cutting wood for a new barn for Nellie and the new mare. He would have to get help from his friends for the project but they were always willing. Winter was mild that year and he felt comfortable with the progress of his frontier home. He studied the soil and found a layer of clay near the bottom of the mountain that might be good for making bricks. His land did have the kind of stone that the Germans had used so well, and he found that he was always carrying rocks for a wall. Clearing another two acres so Berthe would have good graze was his first goal. She foaled with ease and the young stallion was named Frantz after the German family in Northhampton.

Chapter III

Prelude to War

John and Margery were married the next spring and as the years passed by, were blessed with children and relative prosperity from raising the great horses. They were always interested in the activities of the colonies. John had held church meetings at his home until the group grew too big for the cabin and he was able to build a small meeting house with the help of the neighbors. As children grew older, a school was also built nearby and Margery took over duties of teaching the neighborhood children.

In Massachusetts Colony, public schools for small children had become a mandatory law very early in the 1600's, and a teacher was ordered to be paid for the work. They were soon followed by mandatory schools for high school age students to prepare them for the college level which was, of course, Harvard. By 1776 there were ten colleges. Many people could read and followed with great interest the happenings in the colonies.

Great Cove began to feel like a community, even having a small inn and tavern at the bottom of Stoney Batter Hill.

By 1747 English traders, or in George Croghan's case, Irish traders, had penetrated the French area west of the Ohio, as far as what is now Cleveland, Dayton, and Louisville, and had set up trading posts in these places. The French and English had been struggling against each other in Europe for centuries, even calling one of their series of continuing wars, fought mainly in France, "The Hundred Years War," (1337-1453) Major power struggles would find strange European alliances, some of those alliances put together by Christian countries to repel the Turkish invasion of Europe.

The biggest post that the Irish trader George Croghan had established, Pickawillany, was near what is now Dayton, Ohio. The French, in fear of the English competition, had built a number of forts from Niagara to Detroit and along the Allegheny and down the Mississippi. Croghan's home was called Aughwick. and perhaps thirty miles north up the Cove Valley then over a mountain and along the Aughwick Creek from John Martin's cabin and would have been one of the closest places to go to trade for the goods that frontiersmen needed, and Croghan needed the kind of horses that John Martin was raising.

West of the Great Cove, by about 150 miles and a lot of mountains, a French troop led by a soldier named Celeron arrived at the confluence of the Monongahela and Allegheny Rivers and buried a lead plate that read, roughly translated from the original French:

Year 1749
This is the reign of Louis Fifteenth
King of France

We, Celoron, commanding the detachment sent by the Marquis de la Galissoniere, Commander General of New France, to restore tranquility in certain villages of these cantons, have buried this plate at the confluence of La Belle Riviere (the Ohio) the Kanaougo (the Monongehela), this 29th July, as a token of renewal of

> *possession heretofore taken of the aforesaid Riviere La Belle, of all streams that flow into it, and all lands on both sides to the source of the aforesaid streams, as the preceeding Kings of France have or ought to have enjoyed it, and which they upheld by force of arms and by treaties, notably those of Ryswick, Utrech, and Aix-La-Chapelle.*

The indigenous people of the area were on fairly good terms with the French. The French gave them gifts and traded things that the Indians were beginning to need and did not really move a lot of settlers onto the land and drive out game as the English did. However, the Indians did not want the French to claim Indian land for their own. The French wanted to connect their holdings in Canada with their holdings far south in Louisiana using the Allegheny, Ohio, and Mississippi Rivers.

At pretty much the same time, Thomas Lee, as president of the Virginia Council and governor of the Dominion of Virginia, was posting a public proclamation at Williamsburg, Virginia. It said:

> *The Boundaries of Virginia are the Atlantic on the east, North Carolina on the south, the Potomac on the north, and, on the west, the Great South Sea, including California.*

The many wars that the Indians fought against each other had made them become tribes of warriors. They fought for power, land, slaves, and sometimes it seemed that the Senecas just liked to send the young men south in the spring to kill or capture and enslave the unfortunate Catawba's of North Carolina. The trail,

"The Warrior's Path," that led from New York to North Carolina followed the mountain valley that was between the Tuscarora chain on the East and Jacks Mountain, part of the Blue Range, on the west. Great Cove was, fortunately, the next valley over to the East and so was not on the Indian's preferred trail to the South. George Croghan's Aughwick was a short detour from the valley of the trail and, of course, Croghan was able to trade his goods for the furs that the Indians had been catching during the winter.

The Indian populations kept diminishing as they slaughtered one another. That the Indians became such a terrifying force when they felt cornered shows how unprepared the Europeans were to handle a new way of war. Sometimes a politic chieftain would start a series of meetings with other chiefs to arrange alliances to secure hunting and property rights without war. The Indians did the negotiation with flair and style. The English, especially the Quakers, always prepared to discuss things, would organize conferences and work out treaties with the tribes. That didn't always guarantee that truces and alliances and agreements would be honored by either side.

The Lenai Lenape tribe of Shingas is the one that most concerned our hero, John Martin. They were also referred to as the Delawares, because when our history begins, they were situated in the area between the Delaware River and the mountains when that land was sold to William Penn back in the late 1600's, not apparently by the Lenai Lenape but by the Iroquois who took a sizeable pile of goods and departed happily. The Lenai Lenape said that the land had been sold out from under their feet. The Lenai Lenape were considered "women" by the Iroquois because, some time back, they had lost a war with the

Iroquois. The one treaty that the Lenai Lenape had heard about entitled them to remain on the land. However, as more and more settlers arrived and encroached on the Indians' land, going even beyond the first mountain range, the Indians moved westward and the Lenai Lenape ended up mixing in with other tribes in what is now Kittanning, PA and Beaver PA.

* * *

It was Spring of 1749 when George Croghan showed up at the Martin's door. He refused tea or a smoke with John, standing near the door as if for a quick escape.

"I hate to have to tell you this, but I did warn you. I told you years ago that you shouldn't be here. You and your friends have no real title to this land."

John said, "I've been to Philadelphia to discuss this with the authorities there . . . ."

"I heard. You didn't get anywhere, did you?" Croghan shook his head. "I didn't think it would come to this but I have been told, by the Proprietaries, to tell you that you must leave. This land belongs to the Indians and . . ."

"But I made application for this land from the Ohio Company that is based in Virginia. They said that this land is far enough south to be in Virginia."

Croghan responded, "The Ohio Company is wrong. This is not far enough south to be in Virginia. You aren't even in Maryland. You are in Pennsylvania. What you have to do is bring suit against the Ohio Company for misrepresentation."

"They even say that the Forks of the Ohio River are part of Virginia."

"No. No. No. Not so. They are making a grab for some pretty rich land. Just saying so, doesn't make it so. Anyway my orders are to burn all you people out!"

"The Indians have left. We are not bothering them. They wander through every now and then hunting but they moved west."

"No matter. Take what you can carry and go back to the settlements. You would be safer there, anyway. The Indians are being stirred up by the French and I may have to leave, too. Your Ohio Company is going to make a try at establishing a fort at the Forks of the Ohio. I think that is foolish but that governor down in Virginia is determined to prove that Pennsylvania land belongs to Virginia. Is that a meeting house or church over there?" Croghan indicated another, larger cabin nearby.

"Yes, that is our meeting house."

"Get your people together and tell them what is what. If they don't move out peacefully, we will have to force you all out. The Colonial government is determined that you must go back beyond the mountains. You must be out by 1750. We are clearing out people from the Cumberland Valley and Licking Creek Valley also."

"How could the Quakers do this to us?" demanded Margery, in tears. "We live here at peace with the Indians. Don't they want peace?"

"Not when there is a lot of money involved," said John, bitterly.

"If you are still here next summer, I will be seeing you," said Croghan and heaved himself back out the door. He climbed heavily on to a horse that John had sold him several years before, waved and trotted off in the direction of Aughwick.

Chapter IV

Burning Cabins

It is May of 1750 and John Martin's plantation is bursting with life. His horse raising business brings in cash enough for some comforts, when he can get Croghan to pay for the animals. Croghan is often in debt, near bankruptcy, from giving generous gifts to the Indians, and being slow to pay debts to Philadelphia merchants. John Martin has a fairly comfortable, ever expanding, log cabin which houses his wife, Margery and his five children. Mary who is fourteen is a great help around the house. Eldest son Hugh, twelve, is so good with the great horses that his dad marvels at his ability. Margery spends a lot of time teaching them and other children to read and write. Hugh is a very enthusiastic learner, never satisfied, always asking more questions, wanting to know more. Martha is a bubbling nine-year-old. Her main interest is being assistant mother to younger brothers, James and William, who are five and three. John's younger brother, Robert, has arrived from Ireland's County Antrim to help out and is comfortable sleeping in the loft in the barn with the horses whose body heat keeps it warm. The biggest problem is not the cold or the loneliness or the occasional lack of food, it is the Indian problem. Well, not the way you would think of problems with Indians. Actually, most of the Lenai Lenape had left the area sometime earlier.

The Indians had made little clearings, in the midst of the great dark forest and those glens were very appealing. The Indians were accustomed to growing a crop of corn on land that they cleared by banding trees and then improving their crops when the trees died. They built a style of cabin but never did really understand plowing and planting the way the whites did. Planting was left to the squaws who had limited strength. Actually, John had taken advantage of the Indians' work by moving into a clearing that the Indians had left behind.

Indians would sometimes get together in great encampments to work things out. The Lenai Lenape were upset because the Iroquois tribe, to the north, had sold the Lenai Lenape land and gone north with the loot. The Lenai Lenape protested at one point that the Iroquois had sold "the land from under our feet." When the Lenai Lenape moved west, there were the French who were claiming the land west of the Allegheny and Ohio.

"If the English have the land east of the Ohio and the French have the land west of the Ohio, where is the Indians' land?"

In the Treaty of Lancaster in 1744 the Virginians bought land to the "setting sun," which to the Virginians meant way, way west and to the Indians meant the top of the nearest mountain. That mountain top was one ridge east of the Great Cove.

Since these agreements were made, Philadelphia and Maryland and Virginia had been disputing about which colony or which land speculators would be able to sell the mountain tracts. With the people of Philadelphia, there wasn't much concern for the rugged individualists who had gone beyond the recommended boundaries set by the Quakers. The situation was chaotic and about to get much worse for the Martin family.

When William Penn had taken over Pennsylvania, back in 1682, there had been Germans and Dutch and even Swedes on the land. Penn assured them that the new government would not be a problem for them and it was not. They just re-filed for their land and received clear title. That was William Penn. The Penns, the three sons of William, who now were the "Proprietaries," were interested in making money from the Colony.

"Quakers are great believers in talking things out," said Margery. "But in this case I don't think that they are going to listen to us. These fellows are coming here to burn us out. We will just have to go and leave all our work behind."

"It just doesn't seem fair. It was part of Virginia and I thought that Virginia had bought the land from the Iroquois. I bought the land from Virginia . . . I have a warrant," protested John, but he knew that he was in Pennsylvania.

The warning had been delivered earlier by George Croghan and John had gone to Philadelphia to plead his case to the colonial government, but to no avail. So now, his herd of great horses was moving restlessly in the corral. He had taken four with him to sell in Conestoga where the huge wagons were being made. Only great horses or oxen could pull the enormous vehicles, and actually they required four or six of his great horses but then they could manage the big wagons fairly well on the rough roads of the frontier. He had no trouble selling his proud crop and with some of the money bought one of the wagons to haul his own possessions for a sad retreat back to York.

Margery had been packing ever since the order that they had to leave had come. She packed and packed but she also had Mary and Hugh carry a lot of stuff to a nearby cave. The cave was unusually dry. It was large enough that it would be able to hold a crop of hay along with a lot of household goods. It could hold enough hay for the winter for the horses and the one cow.

John and Robert had plowed and sowed a planting of oats and enough wheat and corn for the coming year and now the bright green sprouts were just poking through the brown soil.

The day came when Richard Peters, George Croghan, Conrad Weiser, James Galbraith, and others with the undersheriff of Cumberland County arrived en-masse to remove the Martin family from their home. They had burned Webster's nearby mill and the miller's cabin that was downstream of the Martin's land.

The family went quietly. They started back the main road to York with four of the great horses pulling the wagon and four others trailing after the wagon. The cow was led by Hugh. As they climbed over the Stony Batter they could see down to the narrows where the grist mill had been. They could see its smoking ruin. They looked back and saw another column of smoke rising and they knew that it was from their home. There were a lot of tears and there was a lot of anger.

Their passive obedience to the ruling was beginning to fade and be replaced by a hard core of rage. The people who made the rules in Philadelphia should not have encouraged the hostility of the Indians by granting the Indians wish to return to their former land. The frontiersmen should not have been sacrificed by the pacifistic, idealistic Quakers. They should not have been abandoned to the uncaring judgments of the city people.

When the Martins met up with the Knox family they stopped and had a few meals and a lot of conversation. Then they continued east toward Chambers Mill. Captain Stewart had not been spared and he and his family joined the group. They went more and more slowly and finally arrived at the edge of the village. There they settled down to await other families.

After much conferring, the group was dividing itself into two factions, those who were determined to somehow go back and reclaim their hard won farms, and the others who decided to return to Philadelphia and find some other business.

"This life is too hard, I don't want my family to go through all that suffering again, besides, I was a merchant before and I can do it again" said Henry Smith.

Many nodded in agreement but most felt like John Martin and the Knox and Stewart families: the Quakers would go back to ignoring the pioneers. The Quakers would rather not hear anything about life on the frontier. The dispossessed settlers would return and rebuild!

* * *

In 1752, George Croghan was amused that the French had put a price of $1000 on his head.

"I always thought it would be the English King wantin to behead me, and here it's the French wantin nothing more than me scalp. At the rate I'm losing hair, the French had better hurry."

Croghan tried to laugh off the fact that the French had also targeted his trading posts in the Ohio country. The French traders goods were shabby and did not do as well in free competition so they had called upon their government to help them along. The French Government was looking for any excuse to establish their presence in the Ohio country.

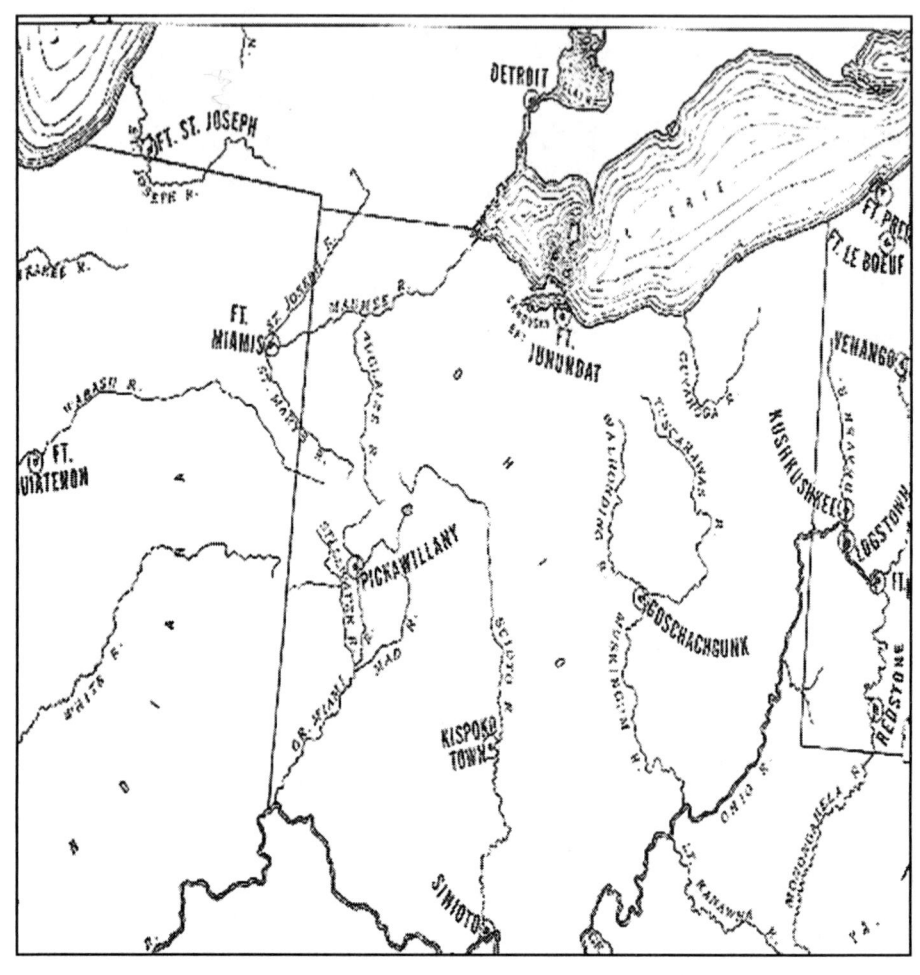

On the map: Pickawillany is near present Dayton, Ohio
Goschachgunk is where the Martin and Knox children
were held: Cochacton, Ohio
Logstown is Ambridge, PA
Kushkushkee present Beaver, PA
Redstone is Brownsville, PA

The biggest of George Croghan's trading posts was at Pickawillany on the far side of the Ohio country, actually south west of Detroit. John Martin had been selling his great horses to Croghan for some time. These and other horses were used carry goods to the far outposts. There could be 80 horses in a line of pack horses. That John had moved back to his land and rebuilt did not matter to Croghan, he had done his duty ejecting squatters from Indian country. Business was business. The beginning of Croghan's financial disasters was on June 21, 1752.

That pleasant morning at Pickawillany broke on a small army of some 180 Chippewa and 39 Ottawa braves, painted for war, and accompanied by 30 French Regulars from Fort Detroit. The French commander was Charles-Michel Mouet de Langlade. Langlade was half Ottawa. The trading post had attracted a sizeable encampment of Indians. Most of the men were away hunting and were not there to resist the attack. Most of the women had been working in the cornfields were easily captured.

There were only about 20 defenders but they held the invaders off for six hours. There was a cease fire called after which the defenders, not having much alternative, agreed to turn over the English traders. Langlade returned the women and let the defenders go. The gristly story of the trader who had been wounded being killed and his heart eaten by the winners was followed by the story of the local chief, Mimeskia, being boiled and eaten by those who wanted to acquire his power for themselves. This savagery was a beginning. The other terrified traders were spared and taken to Detroit. The smoking ruin ended Croghan's biggest, richest trading post and one of the largest settlements west of the Appalachians.

Chapter V

About Shingas

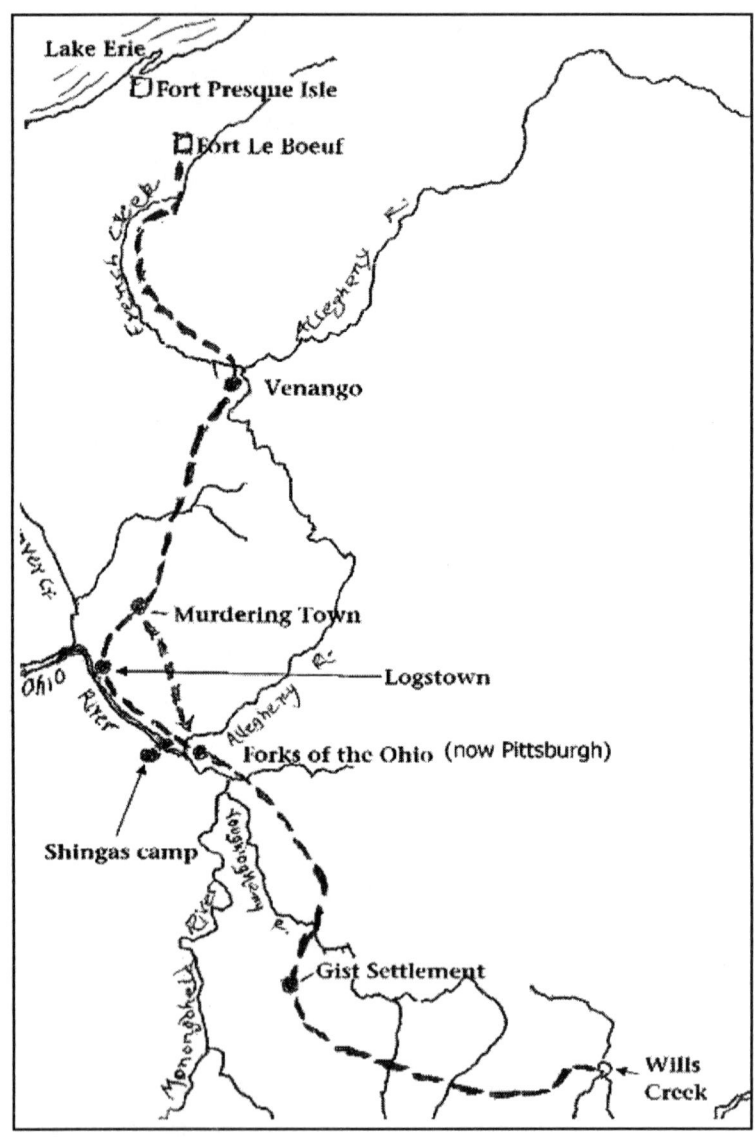

George Washington's trip to Ft. Le Beouf

The prophet and aging leader of the Senecas, Monacatootha, had sent word that a guide was needed for a Virginia officer who wanted to travel up the Allegheny River. Many Indians knew the area well, but none of them could also manage English and French as well as Shingas. He awaited the coming of Gist, the trader and explorer for the Ohio Company and his Officer in his cabin above the Ohio River.

He did not wish to leave his young wife with a sick child. Shingas fervently hoped that it was not the pox. He had the pox when he was a small child and now he could be with people who had it and not get sick. His older son was very strong and had also suffered with the horrible disease and recovered, but with a face that matched his father's in pitted skin.

Shingas was amiable and liked to smoke and talk with the people who had come to his country. His excellent ear for language had picked up not only some English but he also could parley with the French soldiers who had so recently come to the hunting grounds and built forts, claiming the Indian hunting area for *their* King. His Lenape language was similar enough to the Iroquois that he could also manage to debate with the other chiefs when they gathered in the long house to work out strategies. He could discuss a project for hours in the traditional Indian way, but when matters were settled he could also lead his braves.

The group with the officer stopped at the Gist plantation, located on a hillside above the Youghiogheny River. Christopher Gist had acres of land cleared part way up the Chestnut Ridge. Horses and a cow grazed there. It was the first home built west of the Alleghenies and he had talked a few other settlers into joining him in the wilderness. Now that they were west of the mountains, there was less chance of the impending snow.

The very tall soldier was impatient, however, because winter was upon them and a great deal of snow had already fallen on the mountain tops so they started out the next morning. They stopped at John Frazier's cabin and borrowed a canoe for Washington and Gist while the others took the horses over land to the Forks. Frazier had owned a cabin and trading post up the Allegheny but the French took over his property and made him leave. He was also a skilled gunsmith who could make a style of rifled gun.

The last day of October, 1753, Major George Washington had left Williamsburg with a message for the French Commander. In Fredericksburg he had hired handsome Jacob Van Braam, a Dutchman who could speak French as a translator. Van Braam was almost as tall as Washington and anxious for adventure in the wilderness. Christopher Gist. a trader and famed explorer, and four helpers had been hired on at Wills Creek where Gist had another home. These men were some of Croghan's out-of-work traders and one could translate Indian dialects. There was a cluster of settlers' cabins there also, and an Ohio Company warehouse in a fort-like building.

Now they were on an easy float down the Monongahela to the Forks of the Ohio where the Monongahela met the Allegheny to form the Ohio. Washington made a note in his journal that the bluff on the east side of the forks would indeed make a good place for the fort/trading post that the Ohio Company planned to build. It could command both rivers. They stopped on the left side of the Ohio, a short distance from the Forks and, leaving their craft, climbed up the bank to invite King Shingas of the Delawares to a conference at Logstown. The Delaware King had a sturdy log home of the Indian style. There were also several more cabins nearby and snow-covered fields that must have grown corn.

Shingas noted that the Virginia soldier was dressed properly, right up to and including the hat. The hats, that the English wore, always made Shingas laugh. He pictured in his mind, the hundreds of times that the tall English would have had to recover that hat from bushes and trees. Shingas raised his right hand in greeting. The English had to be told to do the same. He did so reluctantly, not looking Shingas in the eye at first.

Shingas was short for a Lenape and had a face that not only had pox scars but had evidence of the wrestling match when he had bitten off the ear of his opponent, and his opponent had bitten off Shingas' nose. He was astonished at the size of the white man and what must be his strength. The soldier did seem to be sturdy enough to be traveling the rivers in the winter. He would have to hurry because the rivers were beginning to ice up. Shingas was an amiable host and they ate well.

Shingas did not like the French at all and was very able to express his annoyance: French goods were shoddy and cost four times what the English goods cost; the Indian did not get as good a trade for his furs as from the English; they, like the English claimed Indian land as their own. Shingas studied the imposing white man. This fellow was certainly well turned out but was haughty. Shingas had to admire the heavy coat and boots that the English wore. Shingas had not seen many Virginia soldiers; this one had something he could empathize with, scars from the pox.

The soldier did not want to waste time being social when winter was upon them. Indians did not favor winter travel but Shingas agreed to at least go to Logstown.

The next day, they reached Logstown. Gist wanted Washington to meet the Half King, Tanacharison, and another chief, the aging Monacatootha. Tanacharison was tall, stately, and handsome. At the gathering in the Half King's lodge, he leaned into Washington's face and told the story of how the French had killed and eaten his father. Shingas and the trader were translating the story and left out none of the lurid details. Shingas expressed the Half King's hatred of the French in very graphic terms. Washington nodded solemnly and hoped to himself that that Tanacharison's story was an exaggeration, that Europeans, Christians, could not allow such hideous savagery.

After a time of conferring, the Half King, himself, decided to head a group of four Indians to help guide the English. Shingas stayed behind, citing his sick child but Washington felt that he just did not want to meet with the French soldiers. They set off over the hills. Days later they stopped at Venango, where they dined with French officers who had taken over Frazier' cabin and trading post.

While Washington poured his drinks through a crack in the floor, the French drank too much and bragged about the great forts and large contingents of soldiers and cannons that would be arriving in the spring. Two days later, a French officer named La Force led them to the large, well-built Fort Le Boeuf which was named for the herds of Buffalo there.

Washington delivered the message from Virginia' Governor Dinwiddie that the French were on land that belonged to the King of England.

The French commander wrote out and sealed a message for Governor Dinwiddie. He did not seem upset that Washington was observing and noting the fortifications and had observed and heard about many new forts and cannon that the French had or were expecting. He knew that the Virginia soldier had learned about the large forces preparing to reinforce the area and more were to come to the area the next year: a real invasion of the Ohio country. He was probably aware that the Virginians would not be able to raise sufficient force to challenge the French and thought that intimidation would be a good policy.

They left on New Years Day in canoes loaned by the French and were able to manage some of the Allegheny before ice became a problem. Leaving the boats, Washington decided to also leave the slower baggage with Van Braam and take a shorter way home over land with Gist as his guide, a mere three hundred and sixty miles for a crow.

Washington skipped going to Logstown to visit Monacatootha again and caused that chief annoyance. Washington proved once again that he was an able traveler during the adventurous return. He was shot at by a French Indian and also fell into a river in the middle of winter and was rescued by Gist who suffered worse frostbite than Washington. They had tried to cross the river on a raft and Washington went into the water. The two spent a terrible cold night on an island but in the morning the river had frozen across and they were able to get to Frazier's cabin. The challenging trek ended when Washington got back to Williamsburg on January 16, 1754. Washington's hastily written Journal was printed up by Governor Dinwiddie and distributed widely, even in Europe.

Even Margery Martin, just a few score miles away from Wills Creek, was able to obtain a copy of Washington's Journal of his trip, and the family read it over and over, enjoying that Gist and Shingas, people they knew, were mentioned. The problem with the French seemed far away from the family. The Journal was used by Governor Dinwiddie to convince the leaders of England that they must repel the French invasion of the Indian lands. The English king responded with a three pronged plan: first, attacking Louisbourg, a fort at the mouth of the St. Laurence River. A second attack would be to Lake Champlain. The leader of the Colonial forces was to be General Edward Braddock who chose to lead 2000 regulars and provincials to the third prong: "Forks of the Ohio" and then up the Allegheny to help attack Fort Niagara.

In the meantime Dinwiddie had, with the help of the Ohio Company, sent a detachment to build a fort at the Forks of the Ohio. They were on their way under Captain Trent when they actually ran into Washington who was returning from Fort Le Beouf.

* * *

Robert Stobo, a young Scotchman who had started a business in Fredericksburg, Virginia, was one of the avid readers of Washington's Journal. His mother was a Mitchell, daughter of the James Mitchell who was hung from a 30 foot gibbet for defending the Stuart royal family. Stobo was also a cousin of Gov. Dinwiddie, and perhaps even a cousin of John Martin's friend, James Mitchell. He asked the Governor to be put in charge of a company and so became Captain Robert Stobo of the Provincial Virginia Regiment. He asked to be the regimental engineer. This gave him a front row seat for Colonel Washington's next adventure.

Stobo's soldiers, collected from the Alexandria area, had no uniforms, rusty bayonets, and ancient muskets. They left Alexandria for Winchester where they heard that an English force of 41 men under Captain Trent which had been engaged in building a fort at the Forks of the Ohio had surrendered to a large French force, at least 1,000 uniformed soldiers.

The Half King and some of his braves had been helping Captain Trent. The Half King made a scene, shouting that it was his fort: that he had laid the first log. The French ignored him.

The English men, permitted by the French, to leave the Forks, did so and met Washington at Wills Creek to tell him their sad story. The French had torn down their efforts and were building Fort Duquesne.

George Croghan told all this to the Martin family later. Captain Trent, his brother-in-law, was glad to have escaped with his life. He and Croghan were partners and had the contract to supply 200 horses to Washington to be brought to Redstone, on the Monongahela where the Ohio Company had a fort. John was happy to sell his latest crop of great horses to Croghan's half-Indian assistant, Andrew Montour, and was pleased to hear about an army coming to deal with the annoying French.

Croghan and Stobo met at Winchester and on May 25, 1755 left for Wills Creek. They were accompanied by newly commissioned *Captain* Montour who had recruited frontiersmen. These particular frontiersmen were Croghan's out of work traders. They were recruited as a ranger group. Montour was carrying a belt of wampum for the Half King from Governor Dinwiddie.

The Half King had sent word that he felt his family to be in danger and was staying with them.

Colonel Fry, who was to be leading this expedition, fell from his horse and later died, leaving the young Col. Washington in charge.

Gist came riding in to great Meadows to tell that a band of sixty French soldiers had threatened him at his home. Half King, Tanacharison, sent a message that he would join Washington at Great Meadows in five days. Gist set off for Winchester with the Half King's message for Governor Dinwiddie. Shortly after he left, Half King sent a message that the situation had changed: he was trailing a party of French marauders.

Washington, with sixty men, set out for Half King's camp on Chestnut Ridge. It rained and the Virginia troop got lost and finally found Half King and Monacatootha's camp. The Indians led the way to the French camp and at daybreak they engaged. After a fifteen minute battle there were ten French dead and twenty-two prisoners. The horror that Washington must have felt as he saw, dumbstruck, Half King disposing of the wounded French Lieutenant Jumonville and splitting his head to wash his hands in the unfortunate young Frenchman's brains. La Force, the French soldier Washington had met on his trip to Fort Le Boeuf, was one of those taken prisoner.

The one French soldier who escaped and made it to Fort Duquesne told his tale to the commander, Contrecour. As Contrecour was arranging a response to the attack, the half-brother of the unfortunate Jumonville, Villiers, arrived with more troops and begged to head the retaliatory force. This was granted.

Meanwhile, Washington had gone back to Great Meadows where Stobo's company had arrived. He felt encouraged by the greater numbers and decided, with the arrogance of youth, to go on and attack the French again. He held up at Gist's Plantation to meet with the Indians. Their news was all bad. French reinforcements had arrived, with ample supplies. A substantial fort was being built at the Forks, and finally, news that a force of 600 Regular French soldiers accompanied by 130 Indians had left the fort and was on its way to attack Col. Washington. This army had already come up the Monongahela River and arrived at Redstone, cannons and all. Washington's people had built an eight mile road west, toward Redstone, with eight miles still to be built. It suddenly seemed that they had been building the road for the convenience of the invading French.

Washington's officers agreed that the best course of action would be to retreat to Great Meadows. As Croghan was later telling the Martins, they would have done better to retreat all the way to Wills Creek. They were hoping to find the food and supplies that Croghan was to have brought to Redstone or at least to Great Meadows but those supplies were held up at Wills Creek. Croghan glared at John Martin.

"I didn't have enough horses, or wagons to move the pitiful supplies that the governor had sent," he frowned fiercely at John. "Your horses would have been a lot of help!"

"They were just colts. They still needed their mothers. So what happened then?"

"They buried a bunch of the supplies they did have at Gist's place. Then they hiked up over Chestnut Ridge to Great Meadows where there was a bit of graze for the horses and a start of a fort. There was an engineer officer who put the men to digging trenches. Stobo was his name. He had to bring up mutual Scotch ancestry to the British officer with the regulars from South Carolina. They wasn't going to dirty their hands with trenching without extra pay. Imagine quibbling over pay when the French and Indians are upon you!"

"Next time you are going to do a battle, let me know in advance." John was smarting some for being blamed for Croghan's problems.

"July 3, The French Captain Villiers reached the rocky glen where Jumonville was killed. I'll bet he was upset that there were still bodies lying there," Croghan went on. "He was only five miles from Great Meadows. I'm told he went up over the ridge and then split his army in three columns. With a force that big, why not? They set up in the forest. I guess Washington was planning on an up front attack that he'd read about in his military books."

"The French did come out of the woods in a line early in the next morning. It started to rain. Our fellows were in the trenches and they shot at the French a bit without doing much harm and then the French turned into Indians and disappeared. They spent the rest of the day shooting from the trees. It started to rain and rain and pretty soon the trenches were full of water. About then I took off. I have never been able to shoot at an Indian. And anyhow, it looked like Washington and his fellows were going to have a very bad day. I hear that one third of his men were killed or wounded."

"You didn't stay to help?"

"Me? I was pretty much in the woods myself trying to talk Half King into helping out. He was feeling very upset. Word had come from the New York Senecas that he was not to help the English. He wouldn't listen to me. Pretty soon he just left with his whole family," Croghan sighed. "I think he's hungry and headed for my place at Aughwick."

"Andrew Montour," Croghan continued, "you remember him, half-Indian, my assistant? Well, he had become a soldier and recruited a lot of my out of work traders. He took his troop clear down to Fort Duquesne to scout it out. He missed the battle, too. His rangers were the only ones who would have been able to help Washington, they know the woods."

Margery showed Croghan the newspaper that had been passed along the frontier.

"It says here that Washington surrendered because his powder was wet."

"Well, you can just bet the Frenchies powder was wet, too. It rained on everybody. I heard that Washington's noble troops got into a big supply of rum and they were drunk. Why hadn't that governor sent food instead of drink? It is just a mess and the worst of it is that Indians like Half King and Shingas will most likely figure out that the Virginians are stupid and join the French. I'll be completely out of business."

"It says here that England might be sending an army of regulars. It sounds like Parliament is planning big things."

"We will believe that when we see it. Well, John. Armies need horses. Get those mares working. I'll probably be looking for horses in the spring." Croghan started for the door, and then stopped. "I didn't get paid for the last supplies that I provided. I don't know how I will pay for the horses but I will surely need them and oats, too. There isn't much for a horse to eat in this forest. Maybe Ben Franklin can come up with some financial help. He seems to know how to squeeze some money out of even the Quakers."

After Croghan left, the Martins avidly turned to the newspaper account.

Margery read, "The action started early in the morning, as did the rain, when a sentry was wounded. The colonel lined up his men in parade formation in front of the trenches, at that point the French came out of the forest and advanced to within 600 yards and fired a useless volley. Washington told his men to hold their fire. Then the French advanced to within 60 yards and fired another useless volley. At this point Washington's men went into the trenches but they had seen the 500 French soldiers with about 100 Indians and the French had seen the 284 English. Then the French and Indians went to nearby woods and kept up a steady, 'galding' firing."

The newspaper story went on to tell of the pathetic surrender of the Virginia Colonel and the generous terms by the French, allowing the English army to take provisions, and even their guns, and leave. There were two officers who were taken hostage, Lts. Von Braam and Stobo. They were to be exchanged for Lt. Force and twenty-one French soldiers captured at Jumonville Glen. Lt. Stobo, regimental engineer, was the one with a sense of humor who named the hastily built and inadequate fort at Great Meadows, *Fort Necessity*.

* * *

Summer turned to fall at Great Cove and the burst of dynamic color that painted the nearby hills gladdened the hearts of the Martin family. Work on the plantation was pushed to make more range for John's plans to raise more horses. He bred the mares as soon as was possible. The herd had grown to be really sizeable, a charming sight when they would decide to run and would flow across the lower field and up to the upper and back again. The hay fields were expanded and fertilized with manure and produced good crops that were painstakingly scythed, bundled, and stacked for the winter. The oats were harvested and bagged in expensive sacks. Usually John would sell off some of the herd but this winter he determined to grow his horse crop as never before.

Shingas came by to smoke and accept gifts. He was very unhappy at Washington's pitiful attempt to drive out the French.

"You know that Iroquois have forbidden us to fight with you? You, our old brothers! We cannot help you. But, if you English do not conquer, if French conquer, Lenai Lenape can stay along the Ohio. You see? If you win we do not have any land. You see? You see what Indian must do?" Shingas shook his head.

"You go. Leave Great Cove. Go to Philadelphia. Settlements not good for family."

Shingas left, saying that he hoped that they would not meet again, that the Martin family would leave and go back over the mountain.

John was shaken in his resolve. He began to fear for his family and the community. Many meetings were held by the people of Great Cove. The Pennsylvania Colony held meetings with the Indians. Affairs seemed not so bad. Perhaps the Indians would at least remain neutral.

In August Shingas had been at Fort Duquesne, seeking some understanding with the French. He had an Indian named Delaware George deliver a letter, from the captured Robert Stobo, meant for Innes the commander at Wills Creek, to George Croghan at Aughwick. Croghan made a copy for Governor Dinwiddie, and one for Pennsylvania's Governor Hamilton, and sent the original on to Innes at Wills Creek. Governor Hamilton showed it to the Pennsylvania Council in Philadelphia. The council then sent Conrad Weiser with three hundred pounds sterling on a mission to the Ohio, to Chief Shingas, to see if relations between the Pennsylvania Colony and Shingas could be made better. Shingas wanted an army sent to the Ohio that would conquer the French. To Shingas' disgust, Weiser could not make such a promise.

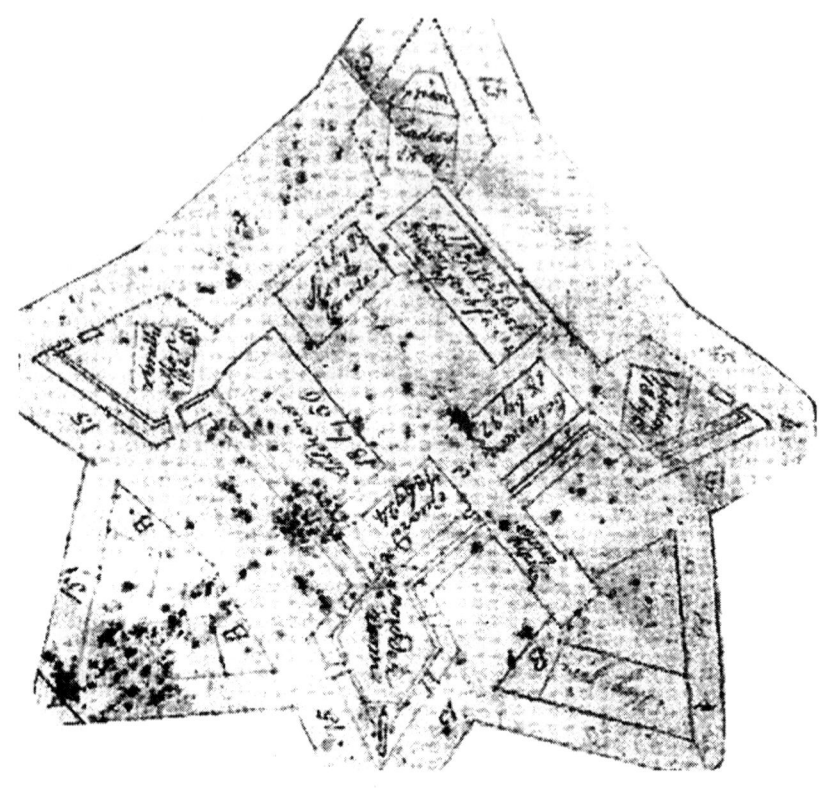

Stobo's drawing of Ft. Duquesne.

Stobo's letter complained that the wounded that Washington had left behind at Fort Necessity, and a small detachment that were to guard personal material and those many wounded, had been captured by the Indians and tortured to death or sold as slaves. He suggested that the Virginians attack Fort Duquesne immediately and explained how with the help of friendly Indians the fort could be taken. Dinwiddie was excited about Stobo's plans but was unable to mount an attack. Unfortunately for Stobo, he refused to exchange the French officer, La Force. So La Force, Stobo, Van Braam and the 21 French soldiers captured at the Jumonville skirmish were in political limbo. When the French found out about the map Stobo had drawn, he was put on trial for espionage.

* * *

John was at Croghan's trading post at Aughwick delivering a couple of geldings when Half King, Monacatootha, and others arrived. Conrad Weiser, whom John well remembered from the burning of his home in 1750, had been there for several days waiting for the conference. John, as a leader of the Great Cove settlement was invited by Croghan to sit in on the discussion.

The Half King had been annoyed by Washington's not stopping by at Logstown after his trip to Fort Le Boeuf. The disaster at "Fort Necessity" had merely reinforced his bad opinion of the young Virginian.

"The colonel is a good natured man, but had no experience; he took it upon him to command the Indians as his slaves, and would have them every day on the out scout and attack the enemy by themselves, but by no means take advice from the Indians. He lay at one place from one full moon to the other and made no fortifications at all, but that little thing on the meadow, where he thought the French would come up to him in an open field. Had he taken my advice, and made such fortifications as I advised him to make, he would certainly have beaten the French off. But the French acted as great cowards, and the English as fools, in the engagement."

It wasn't the speech or any ordinary illness that killed the Half King. He died, two months later, on October 4, 1754 while still near Aughwick. His belief that the French had put a curse on him was his undoing. Croghan had him buried with Christian rites and helped his impoverished family.

* * *

Washington was demoted to captain and angrily retired to be a farmer. His brother Lawrence had died and left him the estate at Mt. Vernon. He courted and married a wealthy widow, Martha Custis. It might have annoyed Washington even more to know that Stobo had been promoted to Major.

CHAPTER VI

At the Battle of the Monongehela
Numbers refer to each days camp

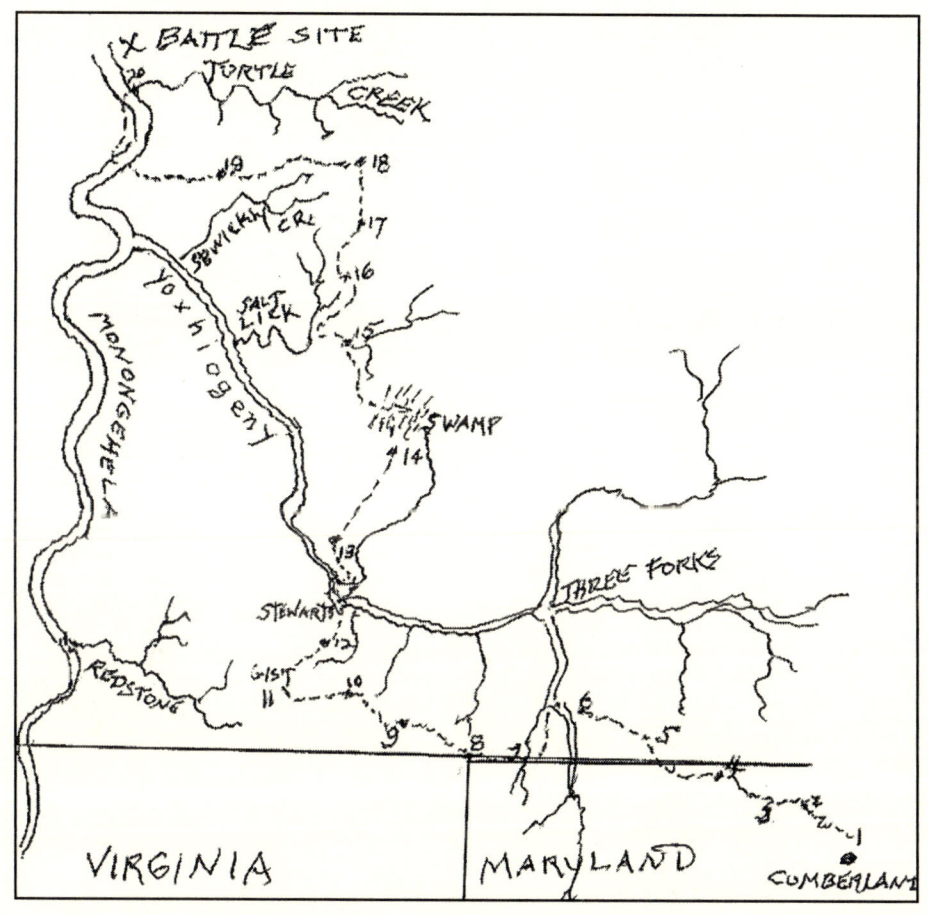

Braddock started at Ft. Cumberland which was Wills Creek
Camp 11 Gist Plantation is Mt. Braddock
Day 12 Stewart's Crossing is Connellsville
Camp 16 or 17 is Mt. Pleasant
Day 20 is present Braddock, Pa

Hugh Martin was dressed in his best linsey-woolsey shirt and pants and they were too warm for this hot July day. Driving the four matched black Percherons who pulled the family wagon was also hot and tiring. He stopped at a creek to let the horses drink and hoped that there would be other creeks with better water for them soon. He climbed down and got a careful drink for himself and sat down in the creek to soak his hat and shirt in the water to provide some cooling for a while after leaving the creek. Across the creek, sitting on his wagon was another young drover. He didn't seem in a hurry at all so Hugh pulled his team up for a chat.

"Are you on your way to Great Meadows?" asked Hugh.

"You coming from Wills Creek?" responded the other lad. He had a headgear made out of a raccoon skin. It seemed a bit warmer than Hugh's straw hat. The raccoon tail hanging down the back seemed to Hugh to be even more hot than necessary on such a day. He also wore Indian styled deerskin pants and a deerskin jacket decorated with fringe. Hugh thought it was a handsome outfit and said so.

"No. I live in Great Cove. Aren't you real hot in those skins?"

"Yep. It is pretty warm in the skins but it is all I have."

"Well, maybe you could do what I did, put your shirt in the water and it would keep you cool for a while. Maybe you wouldn't want to put that coonskin hat in. It might swim away."

"Ha, ha. Well, I just got out of the creek, moccasins and all. And, the hat always goes where I go. See that fellow up there? He's half skins and half linsey-scratchy, like you," the frontier boy grinned showing strong white teeth that fairly shone in his tanned face.

"That is a mighty fine team of horses you have there."

"My dad raises these percherons. They are really wonderful horses," responded Hugh proudly. "We are taking a load of oats to Great Meadow. I suppose you are headed there, too."

"Yep. These nags I am driving were the best I could pick out back in Wills Creek. I just hope they last until I get to Great Meadows. Look at this wagon, would you. If it can go another mile I will be surprised"

"I was too late to see the troops. Did you see them?"

"Yep. One wonderful sight. That line of red stretched for miles. Horses with Officers, Bands playing. Cannons. It just went on and on. I think it is going to scare those French pretty bad. Did you say you had oats? Could you spare some for my nags? They are almost dead of hunger."

"I don't suppose anyone would miss a bag. Have some." The boys unloaded bags of oats from Hugh's wagon and fed the hungry horses.

"My name is Dan'l. There is another Dan'l here, our age. He's Dan'l Morgan. I'm Dan'l Boone."

"Hugh Martin."

The feeding of the two horses attached to Boone's aged wagon occupied them for a while.

"I'm from Berks County, near Philadelphia. You?"

"Great Cove. I guess we are in Pennsylvania. Great Cove is west of the first mountain range."

"I've been there. I've been a lot of places around the frontier. I've met a lot of Injuns, too."

"I've met a few. They were always OK. My dad knows some better. Ever meet a Frenchman? I always wonder what they are like."

"Not very friendly. They find out you don't talk French, they just can't be bothered with you. Here comes the other Dan'l. How about I give him some of these oats for his nags? He is just a hired drover like I am and the army seems to think that feed for the horses will just fall out of the sky. I am mighty glad that you came along."

The other Daniel was a tall gaunt teenager with huge hands, feet, and Adams apple. The hands had an excellent touch with the reins of his team of two tired white horses. He steered them into the creek for a drink and climbed down from what appeared to be a rig that carried a small cannon. The cannon was slung under the wheels and barely cleared the water. He checked the straps on the cargo and patted the horses and then walked over to greet the other Dan'l.

"Did you find something to feed these poor horses?"

"This is Hugh Martin. He has a load of oats. You might want to be nice to him," said Boone with a grin.

"Who haven't I been nice to? I am a really nice fellow," the other Dan'l smiled broadly down at Hugh. "But I'll have to admit, Boone knows all the best people. I'm Dan'l Morgan. Of the New Jersey Morgans. If I had a couple of decent Morgan horses instead of these two pitiful beasts, I could almost say I had a better team than you do, Martin. Are they paying you a lot that you would bring that sturdy wagon to this miserable affair?"

"I hope so. My dad thinks that George Croghan will come up with enough money to make our time and effort worth while."

"I've heard that they aren't even paying the soldiers. How would you like to be marching along, one great big red target for the Indians, and not even getting paid?"

Hugh didn't answer because he just could not think that a year's hard work on the Martin plantation would go for nothing. Boone shushed them and pointed at a tree about 30 yards away. He eased his long gun from his wagon and took careful aim. Hugh was a pretty good hunter himself but until the deer leapt into the air, he had not seen it. Boone raced to the wounded animal and dispatched it quickly. Hugh helped to drag it back to the wagons. The boys laughed and mounted their wagons and traveled to the next campground, Great Meadows. Morgan, who was making his second trip as a drover, pointed out the trenches that had been dug for the battle there. He said that you could still find bodies in the forest of men who had been injured and died there when the retreating Virginians left them behind.

"When I am a general, there will be no such behavior."

"When you are a general we'll be able to eat at a fine table and drink fine wine. I'll be your chef," said Boone.

"I'll supply the horses," said Hugh with a smile.

They had built a fire from wood they collected through the day, and roasted the deer. The activity and smell began to collect a crowd of hungry drovers and the deer was soon gone. Some of the timbers from the old fort, "Necessity" it was called were used to make shelters from the heavy dews. The two boys found one of the shelters and huddled up together. Hugh was amazed to see how much time both of them spent cleaning and caring for their guns, which both kept as near as clean as a soldier would have done. Hugh spent his time before dark currying his horses and hobbling them near the grass that gave the glade its name. He slept near his horses.

There was a beautiful sunrise the next morning. The drovers were awake and lining up to go on the trail that led up over

Chestnut Ridge. The boys lined up together near the front and started off briskly. They had not gone more than a mile than when the first wagon hit a rock that caused its front wheel to fall off. Six or eight drovers hauled it off to the side and the caravan moved on. Morgan yelled to the drover,

"Do you have a gun?"

"No," the disgruntled fellow replied.

"Then you had better just leave it and ride with someone who does. You don't want to be out here alone. Those woods are full of enemy Indians."

"I'll take the horses and head back," he responded.

In the afternoon they topped the rise and descended into what was known as the Gist plantation. Christopher Gist had taken his family back to Winchester the year before, glad to have escaped the French who destroyed his home and trading post.

"Christopher Gist is my idea of an interesting frontiersman," said Dan'l Boone. "He was a guide for Washington. I read about him in Washington's Journal. He knows all these mountains and valleys and rivers. He has been down the Ohio River to the falls. I would like to be an explorer like he is. He speaks Indian languages and knows a lot of Indians. They teach him how to live in the wilderness."

His musings were cut short by a red-coated soldier who came by to recruit men for a burying detail. The three grabbed shovels and followed the soldier. They were shocked to find the mutilated bodies of women. These unfortunates had wandered away from the Braddock's army into the forest and been murdered by the hostile Indians.

Hugh began to understand why the other two, more experienced, boys were so jumpy and were so concerned with their weapons. When they had time in the long July evenings, they practiced throwing their Indian style tomahawks. They were also expert with the knives that they carried. Hugh borrowed weapons and worked on his skills. He had already decided that he should try to catch up with the army and George Croghan. He heard that Croghan and the few Indians who had decided to help the English were out in front of the British columns, scouting. That seemed pretty exciting. Days later, they stopped at the camp called Salt Lick.

It was at Salt Lick that they heard about the death of Scarouady's son. Hugh had met the young brave at Aughwick and felt sorry that he had been killed by friendly fire. The story told was that four soldiers had been killed and scalped by French Indians on the 6th of July. Some of Braddock's Grenadiers went after the Indians. They attacked a small party of Indians. These Indians put up branches and put their weapons on the ground to indicate that they were peaceful but the British Regulars had not understood and had killed them. One of the braves was Scarouady's son. Scarouady had replaced Tanacharison after the Half King died. General Braddock, although usually a worthless old man in Daniel Morgan's eyes, had given full military honors to the dead Indian and a fine military burial, in the British tradition. Then they named their campground for Monacatootha.

"It was a fine show for the Indians. I bet that they were favorably impressed," Dan'l Morgan said. Then he added laconically, "A person couldn't ask for more."

"You're just bitter because you were whipped by one of those darling British soldiers." Boone said it lightly because he didn't know for sure if Morgan might take offence.

Morgan sat with his arms reaching back to see if the wounds were still tender. "I'd like to get that bastard when he doesn't have an army behind him. Did you ever see such a pig, such a clod? And with such tender sensibilities? All I called him was a . . ."

"Doesn't bear repeating," said Boone.

"Maybe it was smashing his face with my fist . . . ." mused Morgan.

The next day was slow getting started, Hugh's fine, superbly trained team decided to do a complicated horse dance and got their lines very tangled. By the time he was ready to travel, his place in the caravan was far back from the other two traveling companions. At mid-afternoon, having passed a camp spot, he pulled off in a creek to water the horses. Away from the noise of the creaking wheels and the swearing and shouting of the drovers, he thought he heard muffled gun shots.

The horse that showed up at the creek had foam streaming from his mouth, around the bit. His saddle was still on with the stirrups flapping. He stopped, breathing heavily and bent his head to drink. Hugh was afraid he might drink too fast and founder so he grabbed the bridle and stroked the nose of the animal to calm him. It was then he saw the bloody spots on the saddle. There was a craze line across the saddle that could have been caused by a musket ball. Hugh took a couple of deep breaths and decided that this was a horse whose rider had been killed. After the horse had drunk, Hugh took the saddle off and threw it in the wagon and then tied the horse to the back of his wagon. He heard shouting and excited yelling among the drovers in the line.

A soldier on a horse that was moving as fast as a tired horse could move was shouting, "The battle is lost. We have lost. Run for your lives!"

His path was followed by total madness. Had you been observing from a hill above you would have seen the main path delineated by the orderly line of wagons collapse and turn on itself like twisting snakes. Hugh pulled off to the side to get out of the wildness and let some wagons go by, headed east. When there was a break in the torrent of wagons that were now headed east, he carefully moved his wagon westward. He had not yet seen his erstwhile companions. He wanted to help the Daniels if he could. The stream of wagons slowed down and quit, some of them looked as if they had been deserted by drovers who took the horses and ran for it. That was followed by a flood of horsemen frantically pushing their horses. Finally one Daniel went by, riding one of his "nags," coonskin cap flopping up and down. The other followed shortly, still trying to manage the affair with the cannon slung underneath.

"Better run for it Hugh! It has been very bad!" He shouted without slowing down.

Hugh decided to turn around, using a break in the frantic rout. He had just managed the turn when he heard someone shout his name: "Martin! Stop!"

He was instantly surrounded by horsemen. George Croghan was there, on a horse. He was trying to hold a wounded Redcoat on to another horse. On the other side of the slumped figure was a huge fellow in the dress of a Virginia soldier, also on a horse and trying to keep the collapsing soldier on the horse.

"We are going to need your wagon, Boy!" George Croghan shouted. "This man is injured."

The three horses stopped and Croghan slid off his horse and reached up to help the injured soldier. Two other red coated soldiers were there instantly, helping. They eased the groaning man down from the horse and then settled him into the wagon, nestled in the bags of oats.

The tall man on the other horse grabbed the bridle of the riderless horse and signaled one of the redcoats on foot to take care of him. That man jumped on the horse and sped off. The tall Virginian shook his head. He took off his coat and gave it to Croghan to cover the wounded man. Crohan held it up looking at the holes torn in the jacket during the fight back beyond the Monongehela.

"Well, they missed you, did they?"

The Virginian gave a rueful laugh.

"Only just missed me. I think I wasn't hit."

More foot soldiers were now coming up on the wagon.

"Turn around and fight!" Croghan bellowed at them. He brought the whip down on a couple of fleeing men and then gave it up as useless.

At some point they were joined by a cavalry officer who was also trying to stop the stampede. The tall Virginian rode his horse beside the wagon and threatened anyone who approached it. Hugh began to suspect that he might be Washington.

Hugh kept protesting the commandeering of his rig. Croghan just shouted:

"Shut up, will you! Just shut up!"

"I have delivered the oats to you. I'll need you to sign for them," Hugh protested, "My dad would want you to sign for them."

"Are you some kind of blithering idiot?" said Croghan in a low hiss. "Do you not know that the poor blighter in your wagon is General Braddock?"

"He's in bad shape," admitted Hugh. "Was he wounded in the battle?"

Croghan, still breathing hard, shifted his hold on the reins and looked at Hugh.

"Him and hundreds of others. We was slaughtered."

The Virginian threatened a soldier who was trying to take the horse that was tied to the back of the wagon, raising his sword.

"If you want that horse back there, you had better put your butt on it," growled Croghan. "You get on home. Your mother would lay me out with a thick club if I let anything happen to you." Hugh crawled back in the jolting wagon, past the wounded man.

"Take me back! I want to be with my men!" cried the General, his face grotesque with blood and sweat. He grabbed Hugh's sleeve and then cried with pain. "Take me back."

Hugh pried the desperate man's strong hands from his sleeve and continued his crawl down the wagon. Croghan had eased his pistols in their carrier to make sitting on the bench of the wagon a bit more comfortable. Just as Hugh was letting himself down from the back of the wagon, the wounded man reached for the Crohan's guns. Croghan felt the movement and tried to grab them. The General begged him for bullets and powder. Croghan did not answer. He grabbed his pistols back and turned back to driving the horses muttering,

"Tis God's law that you go when He thinks best."

He turned to the wounded man and yelled, "When HE thinks best. You don't get to choose, General."

Hugh gasped in horror when he realized that the poor man wanted to kill himself. He managed to get the saddle out of the wagon but it fell and was left behind as the speeding wagon rolled on. When there was a break in the streaming horde, he released the horse from the back of the wagon and made his way to the north side of the trail and into the woods. He knew that if he slipped into the forest the mass of terrified soldiers would soon forget him and lose any idea of taking his horse but on the other hand, he might risk hostile Indians there. He knew he would be more comfortable in the forest.

He made a careful camp that night with the horse after riding east as fast as the thick forest would permit. The next day, after riding east for another half day, he met up with "Captain" Andrew Montour and his band of out of work traders and frontiersmen. By this time he was plenty hungry.

Andrew usually had a few paint marks on his face but he was really painted up now. His scalp-lock was brilliantly feathered and decorated. His mother was Indian and his father French Canadian and he had been blessed with an innate ability for languages and business. They were headed toward Wills Creek also. They told of having been scouting, using the Nemacolin trail, they had reached the hills that looked down on Fort Duquesne. They saw the last of the French troops starting east and tried to get back to warn Braddock but they were too late, the battle was on and the British seemed to be trying to arrange themselves as targets for a shooting match. They were shocked but not surprised that the General had been injured. It seemed beyond all reason how the British just kept marching into sure death.

Montour's troop was still too leery of being shot for savages by their own people to try to use the main road. Hugh told them about seeing Croghan. He said that the trader had been up in front of the expedition, scouting. Croghan felt that when he first saw the hostile Indians and they saw him with his little band of Mingos, they didn't shoot because they were brother Indians. They must have seen Croghan and said, "Oh, look, the guy from the trading post," totally forgetting that the French had put a high price on Croghan's head. He and his bunch didn't shoot at the hostiles, kept their mouths shut, and were permitted to pass through their lines and escape into the forest. How Croghan ended up helping Washington help Braddock was probably an interesting story. Hugh fell in line with Montour's other frontiersmen and eventually arrived at Wills Creek. From there it was a two day ride to his home in the Great Cove.

Chapter VII

The Raid

November 1, 1755 was the pivotal day. Young Hugh Martin was a sturdy seventeen years old. His mother, Margery, said that she had seen a lot of Indian activity in the area and she was concerned. She told Hugh to go to Captain Stewart's place to suggest that the two families get together and go to the blockhouse for protection. Actually, Margery had been packing whenever time could be spared from the harvesting. Word had come in late September that the Indians had been attacking the Virginia frontier. That seemed far away but the residents of Great Cove had also heard that Shingas, King of the Ohio Delawares had vowed to kill every white man.

"We, the Delawares of Ohio do proclaim War against the English. We have been Friends many years, but now we have taken up the Hatchet against them, and we will never make it up with them whilst there is an English man alive," said that angry chief.

John had gone to Philadelphia to try to reclaim the team of Percherons and the family wagon that had been commandeered by George Washington and George Croghan as well as to sell this year's crop of horses and get supplies for the winter ahead. He planned to stop at a German farm near York and ask if his family could live there until the Indian problem was settled. Croghan had come by earlier and had not apologized for taking the wagon but had written a message explaining that the horses and wagon belonged to John Martin. With the hope that he would find his team and wagon, John had gone to Philadelphia where the remnants of Braddock's army had fled after the crushing defeat.

To the derision of the colonials, Colonel Dunbar, who became the one in charge after Braddock's death, had ordered an army into winter quarters in Philadelphia. It was August. The colonials felt that, perhaps, the army could still have defeated the French because there were still over one thousand men. A lot of them were sick. They didn't have a camp. They were quartered in the homes of indignant Quaker pacifists. Franklin was able to quarter some of them in a newly finished hospital.

* * *

Hugh was running like an Indian, one foot directly in front of the other. He knew that the Indians were really good at this. There could be one hundred Indians or two Indians, you couldn't tell because each Indian put his foot where the Indian ahead's foot had been. The rough road that connected the Martin cabin with the Stewart's was covered with the bright leaves that had fallen. Most of the leaves were down now and Hugh loved to see the high hills that seemed to surround the Great Cove. Hugh had climbed the hills many times, hunting deer with his father. He had a well-earned awe of their strength and ruggedness. They seemed to protect the valley, to hang over and shelter it. He knew that was not a true feeling. Hadn't they been burned out once? And now the family was planning to flee east because of the Indians. The valley narrowed a bit and then stretched away toward the north, to the major Indian trails that went east-west through the mountains, following the rivers. There were many Indian tribes to the north, five or eight nations of them. The thought of whole nations of Indians was pretty scary. The Lenai Lenape who had been living here before the Martins and Stewarts and the rest moved in, had pretty much left, going on, to the north and west. They had been peaceful and had had small fields where they grew corn. They picked and dried berries and fruit and nuts from the local trees. Hugh's dad said that the Indians just never really had enough to eat. A lot of their diet was the birds and animals that were in the forest. Hugh never did see a lot of animals in the forest but there were certainly lots that came to eat from the Martin's kitchen garden.

He as he ran along the path kicking up the leaves to enjoy their colors he suddenly remembered that he should be worried about Indians. He and his brothers had always played "hide from the Indians" by burying themselves in leaves under an old fallen tree. The leaves would blow along for a while and then collect behind the fallen log, making a great crawl-space and a snug burrow. A branch snapped underfoot with a loud bang and he felt very guilty because an Indian would never do that. Hugh began to smell the Stewarts' fire. They had a lot of hemlock trees around their cabin and their fires always had a piney smell. The old musket that he carried was getting heavy and he shifted to the left shoulder to give the right a rest. His adventure with the Braddock army had pretty much faded as day to day chores and the moving work took over his life.

When Hugh arrived at Captain Stewart's house, he was stunned to see that the cabin was in flames. He searched the area but there was no one there. The animals, chickens, pigs, and the old cow were slaughtered and blood was everywhere. When the realization that this was an Indian raid struck him, Hugh turned around and ran for home, his heart pounding.

What he feared as he neared his cabin was that it, too, was in flames. He crept up behind a fallen log and burrowed into the leaves. A large Indian party was dragging his family away: His mother was carrying his little sister Janet, age two; his older sister, Mary had his little brother Willie by the hand, and Martha, aged twelve, was trying to shush ten year old Jamie and drag him along after their mother. The raging, whooping savages threatened the helpless woman and children, grabbing their hair and demonstrating how the terrified children would be scalped. He tried to count how many Indians there might be there without revealing his hiding place. It seemed that there were more that thirty braves.

The Martins had heard that captured teenage boys and men were nearly always killed but, often, the white women and children were captured and pressed into slavery just like what happened when Indians captured Indians. Hugh felt that there was no help he could give to his family. He would only die if he tried to help against the thirty Indians in this group. He stayed in the leaf pile by the big log and burrowed down. He lay there a long time with his face in the leaves, trying to not make any noise. It had happened before. The cabin had been burnt by George Croghan. His family was all right. They had survived. They rebuilt the cabin. They would all be fine one day.

The one short, strong Indian was painted half white and half black. This Indian seemed to be in charge. He got off his horse and helped Mary and little William up on the Nellie, the horse. That made Hugh almost angry enough to go after the black and white Indian but he forced himself back into the leaves again.

The whooping of the Indians stopped as they loaded the smaller children on horses and the terrified mother shushed her children and ordered them to do as they were told. They took what food and blankets they could carry and gradually disappeared into the forest. Finally, except for the crackling of the fire, all was silent.

Then, Hugh, with tears in his eyes and a pounding heart, headed toward Philadelphia hoping to meet his dad on his way back to recount the horrible events that had just occurred.

After several days, Hugh found a small barn where he slept, exhausted, in the hay. Then next morning, a small horse was there, and still, no one else was around. Hugh found a piece of rope, fashioned a halter and took off to meet his father. Later that same day, he met three men on horseback. One of the men said,

"What is your name, son, and why are you riding my horse?"

Hugh related the circumstance of the Indian attack, adding, "I'm sorry that I took your horse. You can have it back right now."

The owner said,

"Young man, you can keep the horse for now. Meet up with your father and leave the horse at my barn on your way back."

"I am most grateful to you, Sir," Hugh responded. "I will do just that."

"By the way," the man said, "I was never able to tame that horse. How did you manage that?"

"My dad has always said that I have a way with horses. We raise the great horses. My dad has taken some of them to Philadelphia to sell," answered Hugh.

"Well, I'll look forward to being able to ride my own horse after you have tamed him," the man chuckled.

Hugh eventually encountered his father who had recovered the family wagon and the team of black Percherons. The wagon was stuffed with supplies.

"Well, Hugh. What are you doing here?" a surprised John wanted to know.

Hugh didn't respond until he had tied his pony to the back of the wagon and climbed up beside his father.

"There isn't much rush to get home, Dad."

"Well, I will be glad to get there. What's the problem?"

"Well, the cabin caught fire and burned."

"How did that happen? Is everyone all right?"

"Yes, they all got out of the cabin."

"Well, that is a relief. How did it happen?"

"They burned it on purpose."

"What in heavens name are you talking about, the Quakers? The Quakers came back and burned the cabin?"

"No. Not the Quakers."

John rode on for a minute or two in silence, trying to put Hugh's Spartan tale together.

"The neighbors?"

"Not exactly."

A feeling of dread poured lead into John's chest.

"What you don't want to tell me is that Indians burned the cabin!"

"That is right. Indians burned the cabin."

"But everyone is all right. Your mother?"

"She is alright. The kids are alright."

"Where are they?"

"I don't know."

"The Indians took them?"

"Yes. They are with the Indians."

"Oh. My God!" John's anguished cry took his only air and he folded up and would have fallen from the wagon if Hugh had not caught him. Hugh halted the wagon and eased his father down to the ground. They sat there, holding each other, rocking and shaking with tremors for some time. Finally John collected himself.

"We have to go after them."

"We can't. There were 30 Indians. The leader was painted half black and half white."

"I think that that is my old smoking buddy, Shingas. I heard that he is king of the Delawares since the old chief passed on. Just maybe he didn't kill the family because he has been a guest at our cabin." John sighed. "Who can understand savages? He might think he is doing us a favor to kidnap the family instead of killing them. I thought of him as a friend. I gave him any present he wanted. I just don't understand. We'll get the neighbors, they will help."

"I don't think so."

"Why not?"

"There aren't any neighbors."

This new information was followed by a long silence.

"They were all burned out, too?"

"Burned out or worse."

"The whole community?"

"I didn't see anyone alive."

There was another long silence. John got up and climbed back on the wagon. Hugh climbed up also. They started the wagon moving slowly. Not much was said from there on. Both of their minds were racing, full of "What if . . . ."

Finally, John said, "Son, we will rebuild the cabin. We have to be there if the family manages to escape."

When they arrived at the Great Cove plantation, part of the cabin remained unburned. John and Hugh still puzzled over what the Indians had taken from the cabin and why they had taken the children and their mother and not just killed them. They knew that whites were sometimes kidnapped by the Indians and adopted into the Indian tribe or made slaves. Indians felt that this action was justified because they needed to replace braves that were killed in battle or children who had died. That they took the horse, Nellie, for Margery and Janet to ride was encouraging. That food and warm blankets and boots that were missing seemed proof that the savages wanted the women and children to stay alive over the winter.

Chapter VIII

Great Cove to Kittanning

Margery wrapped the comfort around her shoulders to shut out the cold. She had forced the children, even little Willie, to carry their blankets from their beds. They rolled the blankets up into a long roll and slung it over their shoulders as Margery had seen soldiers do. She made each one carry a cooking pot. Willie wore his like a hat, making the others smile even in their misery.

"We are going to be slaves for the Indians. Just do as you are told. Keep a smile on your face. Don't lag behind. Don't whine. And pray."

There was no time to do more or say more. The Indians pushed and prodded the mother and her children into the forest. With legs heavy with apprehension, they forced themselves to obey their captors.

Mary carried a bag of corn meal over her shoulder and Margery had another bag of meal on Nellie with Little Janet who, being only two years old, was riding the horse. They made their way north, about eight miles by Margery's guess. She tried to be observant and learn enough about the route that she would be able to find her way back when she could escape. She knew that the time would come when the captors would get careless and she would be able to slip away. But, how could she escape? She could not leave her children.

One of the Indians would grab Willie and throw him on his back when they came to the creeks. Willie was both frightened and entertained.

"Do it again," he would cry to the Indian, his tousled blond hair getting a bit smeared with the colors from the Indian's paint.

When they stopped for the night, the Indians would not let them have a fire so they moistened the meal and chewed on small bits of it for a long time. The Indians spread down a blanket and had the young children and women lie on it. Then they laid down another blanket over top of them. The warriors laid close by so that no one could get up without being noticed. Sometimes during the day, Margery would see fiddle head ferns, and as it was easy to pick the ferns and keep on walking, they would chew on the wild plant. There wasn't much growing in November. The killing frost had come and gone and now was what everyone called Indian summer, a bit of a warm spell before the snows of winter came. Settlers would come to dread "Indian Summer" because it meant the Indians might still come raiding.

The leader, Shingas, had taken most of the braves and gone. They did not come back that night. The next morning the group was awakened and pushed along the base of a mountain and then they started to climb. It was exhausting but they trudged onward. Janet was a brave little trooper, not crying or whining. She would slide down off Nellie and walk and the boys would be able to put their loads on the patient horse for a while. Margery began to worry about Nellie. The Indians did not seem to understand that she needed food and water. When evening came the second day, Shingas and his braves brought more prisoners. Margery recognized Susanne Knox and her four children.

Robert and his three sisters were in great distress. They cried and cried and the braves would threaten them with their axes. Susanne was no better. She was trying to smother her sobs. One Indian shook her until it seemed her neck would break. Mary ran to Susanne and yelled at the Indian to leave her alone. She put her arm around Susanne and comforted her and tried to stop the sobbing.

"Hush, hush. Shussh. You must get yourself under control." She rocked the woman and patted her back and stroked her hair.

"You must calm down. They will kill you if you keep doing this. They will kill your children. You must be strong."

"I am not strong. I never wanted to come here. I hate the forest. I hate William. I hate . . ." Mary, fearing what might come next, put her hand over Susanne's mouth.

"I know. I know. This is just terrible and we are all in trouble. It is awful. Just awful. But we are still alive and the men will come save us." This last she whispered in Susanne's ear.

"We just have to survive until they come."

Susanne's sobbing slowed down and became hiccupping breaths. Her children gathered around, frightened by their mother's despair.

"Don't cry Momma."

Soon the rest of the Martin family had joined in the sad group and were offering tiny shreds of consolation.

"They won't kill us. They want us for slaves. We can work. We can do that. We can still be alive."

"Where is your Daddy?" Susanne wanted to know. Where is Hugh?"

"They weren't home when the Indians came," answered Margery. Where is your William?"

"He was hunting." Susanne started to sob again. "There were two fellows, people who had met William, were at our house. They had come to share in our Sunday Service. Oh, it was so terrible!" She choked up and could not talk. After some calming from Margery, she continued, "Early Sunday morning, the dogs started yapping outside. The two men went to the door to see what was causing the excitement. They went to the door. I was just working on breakfast. I was just over by the fireplace. The one fellow opened the door and stuck his head out. It seemed safe so he started out with the other fellow close behind him." she whispered. "I heard a shot and the one fellow fell. I told the other fellow to close the door. When he tried to drag the first one's body inside, he was shot, too. He fell on top of the first man. I tried to get to the axe, but before I could get it, that big Indian was inside. He grabbed my arm and dragged me out the door. He threw me so hard that I hit against a tree and was knocked fuzzy. I just sat there in a daze and watched them grab the children and scalp those two poor fellows. See, that is the one's red hair."

She pointed at a tall brave who was standing guard. The red hair scalp ended in a piece of red flesh. The Indian had it tied to his breech cloth but had taken it and shown it to his fellows and told a story about it. The other Indians whooped to congratulate him. Susanne sobbed again.

"Your William and my John will come for us," said Margery. "You will see. They just need to get more help. We must be grateful that they weren't home and killed like those two unfortunate fellows who were at your cabin. There are an awful lot of Indians here. But there are a lot of our frontiersmen, too. They just need to get together and come for us. And they will. You'll see."

Susanne was calmer. She began to murmur about the family's fine china that the Indians had destroyed, that could never be replaced. She muttered on and on about her fancy clothing that was gone. She listed the household items right down to the butter churn that were gone. Margery realized that Susanne could not face the reality of the capture. She put her mind away from the danger to her children by fussing about lost possessions. She drifted off to an exhausted sleep before she got around to the dogs and the two unlucky visitors again.

The next day they resumed their dreary march. On the up hills Margery would tell the children to use baby steps but a lot of them. They were bravely trying their best but would have to stop and rest from time to time. The Indians would pick branches and switch them onward.

They were joined by other captives, stunned, desperate women and children. The group became larger and slower. They came to the smoldering remains of a cabin where the entire family had been killed and scalped: the sight, too awful to look at, and yet they could not look away. Other scenes of burned cabins and the sinful treatment of the frontier people were observed as they continued north, on down a stream. They came to a place that people whispered,

"That is, was, Rays. That was a store."

Horrible, bloated bodies lay around the devastated buildings. The Indians had even killed horses and live stock and they, too, were rotting in the sun. The prisoners trudged on.

"We are alive," Margery would say to them. "Be strong. God has something better for us. We can survive. We are God's people. Yes, even though I walk through the valley of the shadow of death, I will fear no evil. Repeat it after me!"

The children would dutifully repeat the line by line: the stumbling, sad psalms.

The Indians had paused long enough to light a fire and singe the hair of a hog that they had brought from a farm and roasted the meat. They roasted the chickens and turkeys that they got there for the prisoners. Some of the scalps that they had acquired were carefully dried by the fire. There were even a few green apples. Then they hurried the captives on north, up the valley. There was a Frenchman now with the group, a soldier. When the warriors went off on raids, the Frenchman went with them. The next few days they had tried to eat the deer that the Indians shot but could just barely get it down with no bread or salt. Sometimes they would be given time to gather whortle-berries that had dried up on the bushes. The tiny wild grapes that grew everywhere were worth the sucking on then and the spitting out of the seeds. One of the next days it rained the entire day. The Indians made tents out of some extra blankets. Everyone clung together between two more blankets. When they awoke the next morning, the rain had turned to snow. The golden forest that they had been almost enjoying because of its beauty was laden with the wet, heavy snow that made the ground a slippery trial. The travel became even more difficult but at least the horse could now get moisture from the snow. She chewed on the leaves and twigs of the black birch trees that were brought low by the weight of the snow.

The morning before they arrived at Kittanning, the boys were singled out and the Indians pulled all the hair out of their heads except for a small spot on the crown which was left. A wildly dressed Indian with ferocious painting grabbed each boy by the arm, in turn and threw the boy from side to side. After that they tied a bunch of hawk feathers to the top knot and shouting halloos, one each for each scalp and prisoner, entered the camp in a triumphal parade. The camp held a number of log cabins, built in the Indian style. They went to the largest cabin. Inside this cabin were many warriors and Chief Jacob. The warriors each told their stories of conquest. When this story telling was done, Chief Jacob took wampum from a bag and put it around Willie's and Jamie's necks. The other little boys received the same gifts.

When they went out of the big cabin, the little boys came to lines of many Indians lining both sides of a path to see them as they went along. Some shoved in little Indian boys to hit them but the Indian boys seemed reluctant. They then went back into the big lodge and joined the other boys, to be given to deserving families who needed to have young people, coming along.

The rest of the people were also parceled out to Indian families. Margery and little Janet were given to a family who had lost a child to the winters' illnesses. Susanne and her youngest were also given to a lamenting family. The older children were given to families to be enslaved or killed, what ever appealed to them most. Little ten-year old Jane Knox was given to a brave because he had lost a brother during the battle of the Monongahela, one of very few Indians to fall during that great victory.

This brave was very upset because instead of being given an adult white man to kill, he was given scrawny, little Jane Knox. Moaning and singing all the time about how badly he was treated by the chiefs, he decided to take his resentment out on poor Jane. He tied her to a large stump and walked backward with his tomahawk, narrowing his eyes, staring at Jane who was screaming in terror. He paused momentarily then with a loud scream, he quickly threw the tomahawk at Jane, missing her head by inches. The entire Knox clan set up a clamor of screaming and shouting. The brave smirked at their anguish and went up to the stump, retrieved his axe and repeated the performance two more times, now missing deliberately to encourage the distress of Jane and her family.

From the crowd of squaws, one old squaw, pushed her way to the beleaguered little girl and stood in front of her, squarely facing the brave. She said something in her language that the family did not understand but they could see that the old woman had saved Jane's life. She pointed to the child and motioned the brave to let her go. He looked even angrier but he did go to Jane, untied her, and dragged her over to the squaw and threw her to the ground in front of the old woman. Tribal law was that a live slave was better than a dead prisoner.

Chapter IX

At Kittanning

Mary Martin was in the bloom of youthful beauty. She had a steady boyfriend, David, who would come "sparking" after the church service on the Sundays when the circuit rider would come by. Now, she was very unhappy that she had attracted the attention of more than one of the Indian braves. They often contended with one another as a sport but now they contended with each other for the chance to have the blue-eyed blonde for a wife. Mary had suffered more than the others on the trek to Kittanning because she had twisted her foot when she caught it between two rocks and when she fell, the ankle was injured, perhaps broken. Margery strapped the ankle to two sticks to help to take the strain from the injured foot.

"Don't cry. Don't fuss. Just tell yourself that you don't feel the pain. If you look weak they will kill you," warned her mother.

Mary limped along as bravely as she could, telling herself, "I can be brave. I can be strong. I am tough. I can do this. I can be brave. I can be strong. I am tough. I can do this. I can be brave . . . ."

Martha became friends with Jane Knox, who was just one year younger. They whispered to each other and even held hands as they climbed over rocks and logs. The Indians kept jerking them along and threatened them with their axes to keep them cowed.

Soon, Mary's ankle became so swollen that Margery took enough of the load from Nellie that Mary could ride on the horse with little Janet. The small horse was not doing well either. The Indians did not bother to feed her and she grew weaker and weaker with each mountain, each stream, each place of rubble rock or tangle of laurel that they had to struggle through. If Nellie stopped to chew on grass or a small plant, the Indians would prod her to keep going just as they would prod the people who stopped or complained. When the snow began to fall, it was a long November night. The snowy morning came and the family was huddled under blankets, reluctant to get up. With no food, they started again.

The sixteenth day, it was too late for poor Nellie and the old horse could not even get up. The Indians dispatched her and divided the meat for the prisoners to carry and the skin to Margery. She was thankful for the extra protection but it was awkward to carry. Two days later, they arrived at the camp called Kittanning. There were thirty sturdy log cabins, and fields of corn.

It was a permanent looking village, blanketed in snow. Shingas, King Beaver, and King Jacob all lived there with their families. Some dogs and chickens wandering around gave an air of stability. The Delawares had been living there with the Shawnees only a few years because they had been ejected from the area near the river that bears their name, in eastern Pennsylvania.

The Delaware cabin was made of logs, two posts were put upright and two more upright about eight feet apart. Logs were slid down on top of each other, held together by the upright poles that were set in the ground. Stacking the poles made the end walls. The long sides were made by putting saplings in the ground, and tying the tops together, and fairly comfortable. Bark was used to sheathe the saplings. There was, of course, a hole in the roof to let smoke out. The Delawares were angry about the loss of their former hunting grounds and concerned that they would soon lose this land also.

Things were fairly peaceful for a time, but four young braves who were attracted to Mary grew impatient and the usual competition among them grew stronger and stronger as they fought over her. The Delaware squaws were more and more annoyed at the blatant admiration of the white girl as was Mary. The admiration was not reciprocated. Mary hated the braves. The squaws were jealous of Mary and didn't feed her as well as they fed the others. They assigned the hardest tasks to her. Margery tried to share Mary's burdens and received many a beating for that. When the braves went out to hunt, the squaws would beat Mary. She became so miserable and depressed that she gave up fighting for her life.

One day Mary took a knife and limped away to the edge of the river. She thought about killing herself but just could not do it. What stopped her was the thought that the Indians would scalp her and turn her long blonde braid over to the French for money. She sat there for a long time and then, anger building, sharpened the knife on a rock and started to use it to cut off her hair. Since the Indians used a knife to shave parts of their heads, she thought she could do the same. Bit by bit the hair fell away and she dropped it into the water. She cut her scalp a few times but did not care. Finally it was done. Her luxuriant mass of golden hair was gone and she covered her head with the blanket. She scrabbled back to the cabin and leaned against the wall. After a while she slept, leaning against the wall.

As it grew dark, the others returned from their work. Margery wakened Mary to try to get her to eat. She had not been eating for a while and was frighteningly thin. Margery jerked upright when she saw Mary's bloodied head. She stifled a scream but Martha gasped and started to cry.

"Mary. Oh, Mary. What have they done to you now?" cried Martha. "I hate those wicked squaws."

Margery put her hand over Martha's mouth and tried to quiet her. "Shh. Shh. Be quiet Martha. You will just make things worse. Mary, what happened? Who did this?"

"I did it myself. I know that I am dying and I don't want those savages to get my scalp."

Margery sat, dumfounded, shaking her head. "Mary, don't leave us. We need you. We want you."

She tried to get Mary to eat, but nothing worked. Exhausted by the cold, hunger and anguish, Margery gathered three of the children under the blanket and tried to comfort them.

Willie had been adopted by an old squaw and Jimmy was trying to get the squaw to take him too, so he could keep an eye on little Willie.

"Mama, I miss home. I miss Daddy and Hugh and my David. Why don't they come to save us?" Mary would weep. "I hate it here. I wish I were dead."

"Shhh! Don't talk that way. We will escape somehow. You have to be strong."

"I can't even walk. How could I escape? Mama, I want to be dead. I don't want that Indian man looking at me. I don't want to be the squaw of some filthy Indian."

"Hush. Hush, now. Don't cry. They will kill you for being weak."

"I am weak and I don't care if they kill me. I wish I were dead."

"I'm going to stay close to you tonight. We will hug each other and keep warm. Do you remember the psalm? The Lord is my shepherd. I shall not want . . . ."

"Mama I want to be home," moaned Mary.

"Say it, Mary. Say it with me," whispered Margery. "He maketh me to lie down in green pastures."

"Pastures," said Mary softly. "We have a pasture. I want to be there. I want to see the horses gallop just for the fun of it. I want sunshine." It was always hard to breathe in the cabin because of the smoke.

"He leadeth me beside the still waters," said Margery. "He restoreth my soul. He leadeth me in the paths of righteousness for His name's sake."

"And yea, though I walk through the valley of the shadow of death . . . . Momma, we are there, aren't we? We are in the valley of the shadow of death . . . ." Mary's voice grew fainter.

"I will fear no evil for thou art with me . . ." Margery sobbed silently for her dying child.

They wrapped the blanket around themselves with little Janet snuggled between. The rough hide that had been Nellie's was the top layer. Margery drifted off to sleep, clinging to Mary. It was much later when Jimmy came over from where he had been to join his family. He shook Margery to waken her.

"Momma, Wake up. Momma. Mary. There is something wrong with Mary. Momma. I think Mary is dead."

Margery got up quickly and pulled the Mary's body under the covers. She quieted Martha and sternly warned the children not to make a noise.

"Momma. They will take Mary's scalp. It is worth money," said Jimmy. "Momma, they do awful things to bodies."

"Yes, Yes, I know. What can we do?" she whispered. "We can't bury her. The ground is too hard. It is frozen."

"She wanted to escape," said Martha, trying to control her sobbing. "We should have tried to escape."

"It's too late to think about that now. Try to think what we can do," Margery said, sniffling.

"I've been thinking how to escape," said Jimmy. "I would take one of those canoes down by the river. If you could get out of sight with the canoe, they wouldn't know which way you went."

"Mary could escape in a canoe," said Martha, her eyes drying up as she began to think of a plan. "If we could get her to the river bank, she could be free!"

Margery began to feel better also. "We could put her in Nellie's hide and slide her down to the bank. Jimmy, go see if you can get Susan Knox and Janie to help us. Only if they wouldn't wake up the Indians. And if they are willing to risk being caught."

Jimmy disappeared, in the Indian way he was learning. Margery and Martha put Mary on the horse hide and carefully slid her out the door. Susan Knox was standing outside. After giving Margery a hug, she grabbed one side of the hide and they lifted Mary from the ground and very carefully carried her down to the river bank. Snow was softly falling and covering the small noises they made as they half carried and half dragged the dead girl through the snow. They slid her down the bank to the water. Jimmy, with Martha and Jane's help, had slid a canoe to the water. Then there was a panic when Jimmy fell in, but he quickly scrambled out and urged them to use the canoe that he held.

"Put her in this one," whispered Jimmy. "I have looked at all these boats. This one is the best. Put her here."

They eased her into the canoe and Susan Knox said,

"We should say some words for her."

"We'll think the Lords prayer," said Margery. They said it softly to themselves but on the count of three, shoved the canoe far into the stream.

"Oh, my," Said Margery. "What if someone sees the canoe and goes out for it?"

"I've been learning to paddle the canoes," said Jimmy. "I thought about that. About how she could really escape. I know the canoes. I put a hole Mary's canoe. It won't go far. It will sink and then she will really be free."

A little light was beginning to show in the eastern sky so the two families, after agreeing on a story about Mary becoming demented and perhaps wandering into the forest, returned to their cabins. Jimmy shivered for a long time but slowly grew warm again. The braves who had pursued Mary were the only ones who asked about her. The squaws seemed to know that she was dead.

Martha had the hardest time recovering from Mary's death. She cried for three days and then she didn't cry any more. She didn't sing or run and jump any more either. She hardly spoke to anyone but her friend Jane Knox. She was 12 and she became a sad adult when Mary died. She decided to learn everything about being an Indian. She had decided that come what may, she would survive. In order to not be such a stand out blue-eyed yellow-haired white person, and the object of anger and beatings, she painted her face and hair red and used black to make a scowling mouth. It took a bit of looking and noticing the blue eyes to realize that Martha was not an Indian.

* * *

One beautiful spring day, when every plant seemed to be in bloom. Everyone awoke each morning to the garbled noise of the birds, returned, and seeking mates. Margery was ordered to go into the forest to look for certain roots. The sassafras made a wonderful tea but the roots had to be dug. Little Janet was not permitted to go with her and the squaws had tied her, for safety's sake, to a post by an aged squaw. She sat playing with branches and twigs and pebbles, looking up now and then to see if her mother might be coming back. It was there that a French-Canadian trader saw her. He was beguiled by her sweet face that was edged with golden ringlets. She looked up at him and she saw a man with a golden beard and thought that it was John Martin. She was thrilled.

"Daddy. My Daddy!" she called. "Daddy, I luv you."

Baubee, the trader, was so pleased that the child had taken to him and wanted to be picked up that he burst into a delighted laugh. He sat down beside the little girl and patted her head. She tried to crawl into his lap but the rope held her back. He looked at the old squaw.

"I buy little squaw. You say how much."

"Me want blanket," she grinned a toothless smile. "Two blanket."

"One Blanket." Baubee stood up as if he were going to leave. Quickly the old squaw relented and agreed to one blanket, glad to have something worthwhile instead of a useless child.

Baubee searched his pack and pulled out a good blanket which the squaw snatched away from him.

"You take little one."

Baubee found another blanket and wrapping it around the child, carried her to the mule on which he had put the year's collection of furs. The child clung to the mule's ties laughing and glad to be riding on the animal, the two set off for Quebec.

When Margery Martin came back out of the woods that day, she automatically started looking for little Janet. The child was not tied to the post and could not be found. One old squaw was holding a blanket to her face.

"Where is my Janet?" Margery demanded. The squaw understood her perfectly well, and cackling, hugged the blanket around herself.

One of the other prisoners told Margery of the French trader who had bought the child for the blanket and left, headed for Quebec. Margery was suddenly so angry that she had trouble controlling herself.

"How could people be so depraved that they would sell a child for a blanket? My baby!"

A chance to follow Janet came a month later when another trader passed through who was going to the French colonies. Margery made a contract with the trader to cook for him, work the furs and in general to pay her own way to Quebec. So he bought her from the Indians and they started north. If Margery was permitted a horse, the trip to Lake Erie would have been not much more than a week, but probably a horse would have been carrying the furs that the trader had come for. Margery walked but by now she was one tough pioneer. The trader had left some a bateau at the lake to carry the furs to Fort Niagara. There was, of course, the daunting portage at Niagara, and then boating along Lake Ontario to Montreal and then by boat again northeast down the St. Lawrence to Quebec City.

Chapter X

At Sewickley Creek

In 1756 yet another peace conference was held. One of the negotiators was an eastern Turtle Clan Delaware named Teedyuscung. Teedyuscung wanted peace for his people and houses and teachers. The conferences at Easton eventually brought a lessening of the hostilities.

"The land is the cause of our Differences, that is, our being unhappily turned out of the land; . . . they do not act well nor do Indians justice . . . We on our parts, gather up the leaves that have been sprinkled with blood, we gather up the blood, the bodies and the bones, but when we look round, we see no place where to put them."

That spring, the Martin and Knox children and other white captives made another trip, of twenty some miles, down the Allegheny to Fort Duquesne, in canoes. There were about two hundred prisoners at Fort Duquesne at that time. The French commander was offering a bounty for pioneer scalps. He had already paid for five hundred scalps. A bounty for Indian scalps was also being paid in Williamsburg and Philadelphia. That the Pennsylvania Council would do such a thing horrified the Quakers to the point that they withdrew from politics. Franklin's anti-Quaker group had won.

The French at Ft. Duquesne did not have enough food for all the mouths and sent the captives along, in canoes, down the Ohio. Martha and Jane Knox and Martha's two little brothers were taken instead up the muddy Monongahela River to the clean, clear Youghiogheny River, and then on up to Sewickley Creek. They stashed the canoes and carried their precious possessions, blankets and winter clothing up to Captain Jacob's Cabin.

It was spring and the children were enchanted with the glory of the variety of flowers that bloomed everywhere. They worked in the clearing, planting the corn, each couple of kernels accompanied by one of the fish from the abundant creek. The boys worked more at learning how to trap or shoot the small animals that came to visit the gardens. On days that it was too rainy to work, they were busy inside the cabin, working the furs to prepare them for the day when the trader might come. The corn grew and fall came and the crops were harvested and stored in clay pots. Fish were dried. Meats of different kinds were dried. Corn cakes were cooked hard and dried. The sweet days of summer were gone and the chill of fall brought a glorious month of changing colors. The old Indian squaws who were their owners, didn't have to beat the children as much as they had before. The children had become reconciled to not trying to escape because they had no idea where they should go. The old Indian trail that was nearby had had much traffic a couple of years before, but nothing went by on it now. The squaws felt safe from marauding Cherokees or Iroquois and seemed to feel safe from the frontiersmen. Chief Jacob came by only once in late August. His visit was interrupted when a runner came to fetch him back to Kittanning.

The winter passed with a minimum of starvation and the flower filled spring came again. That year was very pleasant with good crops and the boys were able to keep them furnished with small game for food.

The boys were beginning to stalk young deer the next spring. They and the girls also busied themselves with planting again but when the first little sprouts were beginning to show, Shingas and some of his braves showed up and urged the children to gather their belongings and drag them down to the creek where the canoes were uncovered from their hiding places and made serviceable again.

The wide pool of the Youghiogheny reflected sunlight glittering with sparkles and bedecked with blossoms that had fallen from the trees. The children wanted the old squaws to come also but the braves hurried them along. As they floated away, down the stream, the squaws set up a wailing which soon faded away.

They stopped at Fort Duquesne and were astonished by the busy Fortress. The many French soldiers seemed to be applying themselves to packing and from time to time, a group of them would push a canoe into the water and start off up the Allegheny. Consulting with each other, the children decided that the French might be about to abandon the fort. They decided that this was a very hopeful sign. Shingas appeared and abruptly gathered them and some other captives and they set off down the Ohio. Shingas stopped in a couple of miles on the left side of the river. He went to a camp spot of his own that had been abandoned some time back and retrieved some gunpowder and bullets. He had been given some supplies at the Fort, but not enough and he complained loudly, saying that the French were being stingy.

They set off the next day and, passing Logstown where Washington and Christopher Gist had met with Shingas and the half King, just three years before, without stopping. They halted at the mouth of the Beaver River. Shingas had built another community there, with the help of the French. Several rugged cabins were on a grassy bluff, overlooking the river.

Where the Beaver Creek flowed into the Ohio, the "beautiful" river takes a turn, almost a U turn and heads southwest. They stopped at the place where the kings Beaver and Shingas and Shingas' brother Tamaqua now lived. Not enough food for them there either. They were passed along, again in canoes, down the river now to what is now another turn south. From there they went overland to the Muskingum.

Where the Tuscarawas River meets the Muskingum River was the large Indian village called Tuscarawas or Tamaqua or Coshocton where the boys and Robert Knox and Martha Martin and Jane Knox spent the rest of the war.

Chapter XI

The Battle at Kittanning

In 1756 Pennsylvania's Governor Morris was replaced by William Denny but prior to leaving, Governor Morris had responded to Benjamin Franklin and Col. Armstrong's urging to attack the Indian village of Kittanning.

Ben Franklin, the leader of the non-Quakers, had backed a forts plan. Franklin had been instrumental in the building of the forts, actually supervising the building of some of them. Now, there was a string of them, about twenty miles apart. Too late came the realization that isolated, poorly manned forts were just juicy targets. A fort with ten defenders holding off forty or fifty Indians, advised by one or two French officers, is not a fair fight; forts and lives were lost.

The attacks by Kings Beaver and Shingas and Chief Jacob seemed to be thrust from Kittanning. That camp was on an old Indian trail that was fairly easy to follow. It was also on the Allegheny River and easily supplied by the French. John Armstrong and Ben Franklin both advised going on the offensive.

When John Martin heard about the expedition, he hastened to join it because there was every chance that his wife and children were at the camp. He and his son, Hugh, reached Fort Shirley, which had been built by George Croghan at his former home, Aughwick, by September 5. They hastened on, passing through "Beaver Dams" where Col. Armstrong's force had collected. They met the huge, wild man known as Captain Jack there. He was dressed in the fringed buckskins that frontiersmen found comfortable. He was in a bad humor because Col. Armstrong had refused his help.

"Ain't got good sense," muttered Captain Jack, pulling on his grey streaked beard. "I'm the best Injun hunter in this colony. I've kilt mebby 20 Injuns. I'm ready to go kill some more and they don't want my help? Am jest gonna set here until the remains of em gets back. They'll be runnin, I'll bet. Then I be up on that bluff there waiting for the Injuns that's follerin them and picking off a few a day, and I'll get me a few Injuns of them picken off Injuns by doin some picken off m'self."

"We will be looking for my other five children and my wife," said John. They were kidnapped the first of November in 1755 from Big Cove Valley."

"You think they are still alive?" asked Captain Jack. "Iffn they are, you're lucky. Mine was kilt right in my cabin. I been killin Injuns ever since. Thet Colonel Armstrong, he don't want me because I ain too kerful about which Injuns I kill. I am just as happy to kill the women and children, too. Jest lak they did to mine. You from Great Cove? Mebby you could help me out sometimes when I go Injun huntin?"

Hugh and John nodded their heads and, without saying how horrified they felt at Captain Jack's confession, moved on.

"He's right about people running back, Dad," said Hugh, remembering the desperate flight of the wagons from the defeat of Braddock. "If Colonel Armstrong loses this battle, it will get bad here too."

"Well, we will just see. We are so far behind that we will probably miss the battle but perhaps we can find out if the family was there."

"I heard that Ben Franklin tried to talk Braddock into using Captain Jack and some of his pals into being guides but Braddock didn't want any parts of him."

"Braddock sounds like a better person all the time."

"He was using Croghan for a guide."

"True. But who knows the forest better than Croghan? Who knows the Indians better?"

"Croghan could only get about 20 Mingos to go with him."

The argument had gone on over a year. John was disgruntled that the British had lost and heaped blame on the dead commander for not using friendly Indians. Hugh, having been a lot closer to the action, was inclined to give the British regulars the benefit of the doubt. So the argument went on.

They hastened to follow the three hundred men along the old Kittanning Indian trail. They learned that they were six days behind the main force but hoped to travel fast and light and catch them in a couple of days. John was both excited that his family might be at Kittanning and fearful that if they were, they might be in the middle of a battle. He was riding Hugh's cavalry horse that had proved to be a strong tough animal. Hugh was on one of the Percherons.

They approached a sentry and were easily passed when they compared mutual friends from Great Cove. The fellow had been recruited from the Cumberland Valley as were most of Armstrong's force. Most of the survivors of Great Cove's gruesome massacre had moved back to the towns of Cumberland Valley and were happy for a chance for vengeance. They had collected quickly and marched speedily through the dark forest. Of course, there were always stragglers.

For some the campaign ended when they got homesick, and turned around and headed back for their closest relatives. Some were so unfit to travel that they began to not only hurt everywhere but to have nightmares about falling into or out of frightening things, like horses or, most terrifying, Indians. The collection that John and Hugh caught up with was camped out too close to the trail for the Martins' comfort. They were plainly rank tenderfoot young fellows. Hugh and John camped in a less exposed area nearby and spelled each other on watch. They saw more soldiers begin to come into the camp and realized that it was the main body returning. There began to be shouts of enthusiasm and so they joined the celebration.

John recognized John Armstrong, the surveyor, that he had known when they were both working for the surveyor, James Mitchell. The Colonel had been injured, a musket ball in the shoulder but he managed to shake hands with Hugh when John introduced his son. He was still so full of excitement from the raid, which had been an enormous success, that he wanted to tell John all about it more than he wanted to sleep.

The night of September seventh had found them, having reached the Allegheny River, creeping north up the east bank. They were attracted by the noise of the Indians' drums, and guessed that the savages were whooping, and dancing. The troop had marched thirty miles that day, and as they waited for dawn, many fell asleep in the Indians' corn field. At dawn an attack was mounted. Chief Jacob responded quickly, sending the squaws and children into the forest. The braves retired to the log houses which had port holes for guns. The Indian defenders were able to fire effectively and kill and wound a number of the attackers.

Finally the attackers began to set fire to the contiguous houses, about thirty of them. This operation did not happen without paying a price in injured and killed. Col. Armstrong, himself was hit.

The Indians faced the burning of the cabins with great courage. At one point, Chief Jacob, their leader, tumbled out of the window of a burning cabin and was killed. He was later identified by the boots he was wearing which had belonged to Lieutenant Edward Armstrong, the Colonel's brother who had been killed by Chief Jacob at Fort Granville. The cabins had been stuffed with armaments and as the fire got hot, the explosions were notable with bodies being thrown high in the air. Chief Jacob's son also appeared to be one of the dead. Armstrong estimated that thirty or forty hostiles were killed.

"Were there any captives with these Indians?" asked John. "My family was taken by Shingas."

"Eleven captives, were recovered," responded the Colonel. "They will be along soon. I asked their names and I'm pretty sure that none of them were named Martin. Shingas and King Beaver were not at Kittanning. They had taken a big bunch of captives down the river a while back."

"Let me tell you," the Colonel continued, "it was a lovely thing to see those houses blow up. We heard that the French had left a huge amount of gun powder and war material. We didn't know that when we attacked. Let me tell you, it was really something when that stuff blew up. Body parts flying in the air! It was a beautiful thing. We counted thirty dead Indians. That was all we could find. We have about that many scalps." The Colonel laughed and then grabbed his injured shoulder. He leaned in toward John and said in a lower voice,

"I think we lost about forty men. You never know. It may be that some just run away when things started. It is bad for them to do that. Those poor fellows will get picked off by the Indians sooner or later."

"So you are calling this a victory?" asked John.

"Absolutely," answered Armstrong with a broad smile. "The camp is destroyed, and their supplies, and Chief Jacob and his son are both dead."

After a moment of thought, he added, with a sigh, "And I got my brother's boots back." John had heard the story of an Armstrong brother being killed at Fort Granville.

"I am so sorry about your brother," said John.

"Well, you must know how I feel for you with your family in the hands of those rotten savages. Check with the captives we brought back, they may know something about your family." The Colonel yawned, fatigue suddenly overcoming his desire to relive the victory.

"Think of how many times we have had a victory against the savages. Not many, or is it that up until now, not any?" The Colonel gave a long sigh of satisfaction, rolled up in his cloak, and dropped off to sleep.

The next morning the troop seemed well refreshed, had a minimal breakfast and set off at the fastest pace they could manage for Fort Littleton. Armstrong had lost many officers and men. Now, he was very concerned about the possibility of Indian harassment.

As they passed Jack's Mountain, John and Hugh looked for the Indian hunter. He did not disappoint them. He came galloping up through the quick moving group, swinging Indian scalps over his head, the red flesh indicating how recent they were.

"I think I got enuf of them stinking savages that they will leave youn's alone."

"Thank you, Captain Jack." responded the Colonel. "Any of them men?"

"All of them men. What do you think I am?"

"I'd rather not say."

"This bunch was sneakin' up on you back at that last crossing of the Juniata."

"Seriously, Captain Jack, I am grateful. We have just a bit of extra food. See the cook and eat with us."

"Alright. I don't expect thanks but I just think you, losing a brother and all, would know that the only good Indian is a dead one. You'll be collecting that bounty that the governor put on Captain Jacob?"

Armstrong nodded with a big smile.

"Seven hundred dollars! Well, what about Shingas? Did you get him, too?"

"No, he is still on the loose. You going to try for the $700 bounty on him?"

"Well, that gives me something to live for." Captain Jack made an elegant display of flourishing his hat, a miserable thing of carelessly sewed skins. He dropped back to chat with the men and try to recruit some for his band of Indian hunters.

The soldiers convinced John that the only white prisoners that they had seen were the ones freed after the battle. His distress at not finding his wife or children was relieved by one of the captives who assured him that his family had left weeks before, going south, down the river, in canoes.

A boy that Hugh talked to, Tommy Girty, told a story about a girl that he thought might have been named Mary Martin. Tommy was a small, painfully thin boy with red kinky hair that stood out from his face. The massed freckles almost changed the color of his skin to brown. He said that she was really pretty and that Chief Jacob's son and others had taken a shine to her, but she detested them all. He said that the old hag squaws would beat her because they were jealous. The squaws were the ones that killed her. Tommy seemed very angry about what had happened to Mary. It was as if for him, the total horror of the tortures and pain inflicted on the captives were centered in the pathetic fate of the beautiful girl, simply because she was beautiful.

"I don't know where I'll go. They captured my ma and my brothers. They was most horrible torturing and burning Tucker, my Ma's boy friend. I am the onlyst one free. I don't know where I'll go. What do I do? I got no home."

Hugh, shocked by the story about Mary, didn't know how to answer Tommy's plaintive question. He mumbled something encouraging to try to help the lad be happy to be with his own rescue. He was too upset about Mary to tell his dad until they were away from the group. He rode by himself mulling over what the boy had said. The kid could be wrong. That poor girl could have been someone else.

They reached Fort Littleton. The Colonel paused there, feeling a bit safer from Indian harassment. John and Hugh kept going and split off toward Great Cove. Then Hugh was able to talk enough to tell John that his oldest child, Mary, was probably dead.

Chapter XII

Margery in Quebec

The Quebec situation was made very much more difficult for the French by corruption at the highest levels. Materials sent by the king were bought by Canadian Commissary General, Joseph Cadet, who had gone from being a butcher to being the wealthiest man in Canada, for 11M from the King's stores and sold back to the King for 23M. Intendant Francois Bigot and the Colonial Minister Vaudreuil were in on the corruption and became wealthy also. After France lost her American empire this gang was tried, found guilty and spent the rest of their lives in prison. They had also tried to squeeze the local merchants and traders.

Louisbourg, the French fortress at the mouth of the St. Lawrence, was captured by the English in 1746 but returned to France by the Peace of Aix-la-Chapelle in 1748 that ended King George's War. In 1758, one of the three plans by the English and Provincials recaptured the Louisbourg Fortress on Cape Breton Island. The effect of this was to pretty much shut off supplies from France to Canada. Canadians were, therefore, poor and hungry. The General of this unusual, winning, British affaire, was Amherst, with a show of brilliance by one James Wolfe. Amherst, after Abercrombie's terrible defeat at Ticonderoga, was promoted up and the command of the force to attack Quebec given to the young Wolfe.

In September of 1756, in Quebec, thirty-nine year old Margery Martin met a Virginia officer named Robert Stobo who was thirty-two. He had been in Pennsylvania with Colonel Washington in 1753. They were both at the Schuyler House where Margery was happy to be working in the kitchen to pay off a debt of gratitude to Colonel Peter Schuyler. Schuyler was a prisoner of the French since his force from New Jersey had been captured at Oswego. He and Stobo were mostly free to roam the city, and Schuyler, who was very rich and very kind, would buy prisoners, considered slaves, from the French or Indians and shelter them. He had bought Margery Martin from a French fur trader, freed her, and had attempted to send word through to John Martin that Margery was in Quebec.

"I remember stopping at the Martin Plantation," Stobo remarked on meeting Margery. "It was, as I think, a couple of days west of Wills Creek. Are you from there?"

"No, we live in Great Cove. It is not very far from Wills Creek, but east and north. We thought we were in Virginia but it seems to be in Pennsylvania. My husband, John, would earn extra money, sometimes, using our great horses and the wagon to haul things for the Virginia Militia. John really did not want to get involved in fighting against the Indians because he had always been friends with the Lenai Lenape. But, we needed the money that Mr. Franklin promised for the use of horses and wagons. Do you know of Mr. Franklin who writes the wonderful 'Poor Richard's Almanac'? He is becoming a politician even with the Quakers governing the Colony."

"Yes, of course. I have read The Pennsylvania Gazette. He is wonderfully entertaining. But, I think I might have met your husband. He is a fairly big fellow with a lot of blonde hair? Did he have a son with him?"

"Yes. That would be my John and my oldest boy, Hugh." Margery gave a long sigh and said,

"My little boys, Jimmy and Willie, are still at Kittanning, the Indian village on the Allegheny. And my poor, sweet Martha. She is still there, with the savages. Were you at Kittanning?"

"Oh, yes. I was just passing through Kittanning on my way to Quebec. There were such a lot of prisoners coming in there at that time. The French sent me here. I have a lot of freedom for a prisoner of war. Most prisoners of war are confined on an island near Montreal, starving, and suffering from smallpox, I hear. I feel very fortunate to be here. I have even gone into business with one of the local tradesmen. We are doing very well. I'm feeling quite successful."

"Even though I am doing well here," continued Stobo, "I still want to get back to Virginia. I have tried to escape but they caught me every time."

He went on to tell her that he had been tried and sentenced to be beheaded for the spying he did while at Fort Duquesne. A stay of execution came from Versailles and his life was spared.

"What is the news of the war? Will it ever be over?"

"Well, the French have a big party and celebrate every time that there is a victory somewhere. So far, they have been doing a lot of celebrating. I have heard that we lost a big fight at a place called Carillon. Nevertheless, I believe that there is hope for us here. No reinforcements have come here for some time. Since Louisburg fell, there will be no more supplies from France."

Margery looked perplexed so he added:

"Carillon to the French is Ticonderoga to the Indians. It is pretty far south of here, on a lake. A large English force attacked and suffered another terrible disaster. The French still hold the lake. Louisburg, however, is at the mouth of the St. Laurence River. Since it fell, very few supplies come here from France. But really, I am very hopeful. Since Louisburg has fallen, it is just a matter of time until Canada falls."

"How did you come to be captured?" Margery asked. "Were you with General Braddock?"

"No. I never met the unfortunate General Braddock. I was with the very young and also unlucky Colonel Washington, in '54. We were west of Winchester. Actually we were pretty far along on a mission to capture Fort Duquesne. He took a troop, about 60, after a French force that the Indians told him about. He ran into a small force of French in the woods and the Indians got a bit out of control and pretty much slaughtered the French troop. The Indian chief with him was named Tanacharison. He called himself a *"Half-King."* Well, Washington must have just stood there dumbfounded while the Half-King hacked the French officer in charge to death. That vicious savage split open the head of that Frenchman and washed his hands in his brains. I'll bet it was enough for a lifetime of nightmares for poor Washington. He was so very young."

Margery had an instant picture of that. She sighed and shook her head in revulsion, trying to shake off other horrors she had seen.

Stobo, enjoying having a rapt audience, went on,

"The French commander at Fort Duquesne was brother of the officer who was savaged, named Jumonville. The brother of Jumonville came out with a large force of French and Indians, steaming mad and ready for vengeance. We worked on a pitiful fort in a swamp called the "Great Meadows." I was in charge of trench digging. I thought I had done a pretty good thing with it but when it rained, anyone could see it was a horrible mistake to be in those trenches. We should have made a run for Wills Creek," he went on.

"The French and the rain came at the same time. It was hard to tell which was worse. Our powder was wet. We were starving and miserable. After a fight, the French gave us a chance to surrender so we did. We were very surprised when they let the Colonel go. He was forced by the French to sign papers about the death of the brother. The papers were all in French, and as wet as everything else. We felt we were so lucky to have escaped with our lives that two of us officers volunteered to go with the French as hostages. Yes. I volunteered. No one was ever exchanged to free me and the Indians didn't kill me. So, here I still am, still a prisoner, a hostage."

Margery shook her head at the amazing story. Stobo told her that he had drawn up plans of the fort called Duquesne. She heard that he had talked the Delaware chief, Shingas, whom she well remembered, into taking the map to General Braddock because it would be very helpful to Braddock.

"In truth," Margery said, "it didn't help much: Braddock met his horrific defeat when he was still ten miles from the fort. Afterward, Shingas and the Delawares went with the French. After the English were so terribly defeated at the 'Battle of the Monongahela,' they would have been stupid not to."

Margery went on to tell about the capture of her family by that same Shingas.

* * *

It was, perhaps, two years later and Margery was walking along the narrow, cobbled streets of Quebec when she saw a beautiful little blonde girl, nicely dressed, walking in the street in front of her.

"Janet!" She called, and the little girl turned around.

"Mommy," answered the child, her eyes wide and surprised. She turned and it was not the tiny, brunette mother she knew, but a tall, bony woman with piercing blue eyes and flaming red hair peeking out from under a bonnet. Then Janet shook her head in confusion. She started to cry, dropped the baguette she had been carrying, and ran away. Janet, in her flight, led Margery to her home. It was a pleasant brick house. Since Janet lived there, she walked right in. She left the door open with Margery standing on the threshold, holding the baguette. A middle-aged couple looked up to see Margery there and asked, with an intuitive sense of dread,

"Who are you?"

Margery replied, calmly, in French, that her name was Margery Martin.

"You have my daughter. This child is my Janet."

The flustered pair wished to deny that. "How do you know?"

Margery said, "A fur trader named, Baubee bought Janet from the Indians at Kittanning on the Allegheny River in the Pennsylvania Colony. For a blanket! He took her from me. I could not stop him. I did not want to give up my child. There was no way I could stop him. I was a slave to the Indians." She towered over the tiny French couple.

The man said, "He told us that you wanted her to be out of the Indian camp and were happy to see her go with him."

"That was a lie," said Margery. "I did not know that he had taken her. I was out in the forest gathering wood. He lied. I want my child back."

"How can you prove that Janette is your child?"

"She called me, 'Momma.' She knows some English!"

"That proves nothing," said the desperate woman, trying not to be intimidated by Margery's size. She stood to her full height.

"It proves nothing."

"Many of the Martins have a birthmark. It is a brown patch inside the right ankle. Janet has that birthmark," Margery stated firmly. Then she stopped suddenly. She did have six children and they didn't all have the birthmark. Was Janet one of the ones with the birthmark?

The woman's eyes filled with tears. She knew that the birth mark was there. Margery realized that she had won her child back. A warm feeling of joy filled her completely. She smiled and cried all at the same time. A long, awkward silence fell. The woman began to cry and then hung, sobbing to Janet and Janet hugged her back.

Margery said, "I can see that you love my child and she loves you. I am sorry to need to deprive you of her. But she is my child. I've come a long way to find her. I want to take her home to her father and brother who miss her very much.

"I have a husband in Pennsylvania and perhaps a twenty year old son as well. There is still a daughter and two sons who are slaves in the Indian camp. Our family has suffered a lot but we each know that however we are tested, our faith in God will see us through."

Margery reached out to Janet. The child moved toward her reluctantly, urged by her French mother. The French couple was terribly depressed but knew that they must give up their beautiful child to this large, passionate woman.

"I'm your mama," said Margery softly in English and then she repeated it in French. Janet, always a loving child, said,

"Don't cry Momma, I love you."

Then Margery really did cry, embarrassing herself. She hugged Janet and the child hugged her back.

"We want to help. What can we do to make amends for what has happened to you and Jeanette?"

Margery said, "I have been working at Schuyler's house and as a governess and teacher of English. I teach children English and now I also speak an Indian dialect and enough French. I am working for enough money for passage to Philadelphia. Now, I need enough money for both Janet and me. What a pleasure that is! I don't know how to get to Philadelphia with this terrible war."

The Frenchman said, "I have an import business. I import many different things from Europe. I exchange furs for these items. Do you know furs?"

Margery answered, "I worked with a trader to get here. My husband, John, used to trap and shoot animals for the furs. I think I know as much as anyone about the value of different furs."

The Frenchman said, "Why don't you work for me? Janette could continue to be with us for a while. You come here to stay. It will make the parting a bit easier. We really want to help you."

So the arrangement was made and Margery paid a symbolic blanket for her child and accepted the help of the French family named Duchat.

In Quebec, Margery Martin and little Janet spent time in Monsieur Duchat's office and storeroom sorting and grading the furs to be sent to Europe as well as inventorying the many items from Europe that were in great demand in the new world. One day Margery happily greeted Lt. Stobo as he entered the shop. His broad grin and great enthusiasm were a welcome addition to the fur enterprise. He had turned out to have an interest in Monsieur Duchat's import business.

Margery asked Monsieur Duchat, "How did you become so fluent in English?"

"Ah, Margery, I am a merchant. Not only do I speak some English but also a bit of German and Dutch. I am an importer and exporter."

Margery responded, "You speak German? I know some German as well since I worked for the Frantz family in Northumberland, in the Pennsylvania Colony. I can't read or write it. My job was just being the milk maid and teaching some English. I worked there to pay off my passage to the Pennsylvania Colony. It was there that I met my husband, John Martin. I miss him so much. He had come to the farm to work long enough to earn one of the great horses that the Frantz family had. He had done so well with the horses. They were a good income. I wrote to him and received a letter back. I am surprised that a letter can get through to John but Mr. Franklin is in charge of the postal system and Colonel Schuyler seems to have ways of getting letters through, so it works. John knows that I am here and is trying to find a way to send money for my passage home. He will be so excited when he hears that I have found little Janet. Our oldest child, Mary, died in the Indian camp at Kittanning," said Margery. She had trained herself to not think about that terrible day but the sudden remembrance welled up in her and it was hard to continue.

"Our next daughter, Martha, must still be in the Indian camp. She stayed with the two boys," she added.

The days, weeks, and months went fairly well for them in Quebec City. Margery never lost sight of her goal. At the end of each month, Henri Duchat would sit down with her and they would go over accounts and agree on the money she had acquired toward a passage for herself and Janet. A land passage through Indian country was out of the question. Margery would sail to Holland and then to England and then sail back to Philadelphia. The Duchats were having a difficult time because the corrupt government made many expensive and illegal demands on the merchants. Canadians were being cheated by their government and were suffering a depth of poverty that they had never known.

Janet, now a pert and lively six, was obedient yet inquisitive and tried to be helpful at moving small furs out to the store to be sold.

The Duchats were more like grandparents, being in their late fifties. The madam put her hand on Margery's hand at dinner one night and with moist eyes said,

"I well know that when the spring comes that you and Jeanette may be leaving us. You know how much we love her and have come to love you also. We will be so sad when you go. She was the child we could never have. Please promise that you will write to us when all the awful fighting is over."

* * *

By spring of 1759, Robert Stobo's two escape attempts over the last two years had failed. But, before General Wolfe's forces arrived, Stobo led eight other prisoners, including a woman and three children, in an exciting escape attempt that finally succeeded in his arriving at Louisbourg.

He descended the St. Lawrence in a stolen canoe until he and his fellow escapees came upon a small schooner. Stobo and his companions hijacked the ship, complete with captain and crew. They reached Louisbourg shortly after the Quebec Expedition under Wolfe had sailed. With barely a pause for new clothing, he turned around and ascended the river, following Wolfe's army in July.

By July 1, a Sunday in Quebec City, the French had managed to get a fleet of eighteen supply ships to the docks at Quebec. Cadet with Bigot's help, in the kind of patriotism that lost France an empire, bought the consignment of stores for 600,000 Francs and then sold it to the King for 1,400,000 Francs. However, the people at Versailles weren't totally dumb and were on his trail.

July, 2, the very next day, twenty some English ships arrived and anchored off shore and offloaded cannon and soldiers. The cliffs that protected the city were an insurmountable defense. Wolfe started to shell the French bastion and it took a toll on the people in the city.

Margery was as frightened as the rest of the Quebecois during the siege of the city. Duchat's home and the warehouse were badly damaged so they all fled to a camp outside the city. The siege was not going to do anything but make the people unhappy because Wolfe could not really surround it. So the siege dragged on.

Wolfe's troops attacked some 500 farms and burned crops and barns to starve the city.

On July 21, Margery and Janet were with Mme Duchat were at a town called Pointe-aux-Trembles, as were many other ladies who had fled the cannonading. This town was successfully attacked by British troops at about 5 A.M. The Indians who were to defend the town fled and the Highlanders and Royal Americans took over, looking for an arms magazine that they had heard was there.

The French ladies with their children were huddling in terrified groups until they spotted an English soldier that they knew: Captain Robert Stobo! They swarmed around him, screaming their complaints and giving anguished cries for help! One of these ladies was Stobo's Quebec girl friend, Rene Marie Duchesnay.

It took a while, but he eventually pacified the distressed women and they were taken down the river and accommodated on the English ships. Their leaving was shortly before the arrival of the French officer, Major Dumas, who had been ordered to drive the English out. This was the same Dumas who had been in charge at Braddock's defeat four years earlier.

Margery never opened her mouth to speak English to the soldiers. She felt she was safe with the French and did not know what her fate might be with the English. The English negotiated a suspension of hostilities and returned the ladies to Quebec.

On July 26, Fort Niagara, France's strongest fort was taken by Sir William Johnson, the former trader, who attacked west from his home in Albany. Then, the French, threatened by Forbes, pulled out of Fort Pitt, and the smaller forts up the Allegheny that had connected it to Niagara.

Later in 1759, about the middle of September, Robert Stobo managed to convince Wolf that he knew a way to draw the French out to open battle. He had sketched a map of Quebec's walls and armaments. He had first hand knowledge of Quebec's defenses. Wolfe had planned to mount another attack from downstream but Stobo was able to convince the general that he knew of a trail that could permit Wolfe's army to climb up the cliffs and have the entire army arrive on the Plains of Abraham. He told Wolf of the footpath at Fuller's Cove, a track that angled steeply up the bluff from the river to those Plains of Abraham situated a couple of miles west of the city.

The morning of September 13, Montcalm awoke to the astonishing sight of twelve British Battalions, in all their scarlet glory lined up, ready for battle on the Plains of Abraham. The French responded with a cannonading which the British ignored. It seemed to not bother them. At ten o'clock Montcalm ordered his blue and white troops to advance, head on, against the British line. 4,500 French soldiers gave a great cheer when they heard the order to advance. The undisciplined blue and white militia ran toward the red line.

"We had not gone twenty paces," wrote one witness, "before the left was too far in the rear and the center too far in front."

All his efforts to restore order failed; Montcalm could only ride along with the adrenalized tide that surged toward the still, quiet, red line of British troops. The battle lasted as long as a half hour ending with the French in total rout. Wolfe, the young British General, was shot in the intestines and chest and died gloriously on the battlefield.

Montcalm, the French General, had his belly and one leg ripped open by grapeshot and died the next day. The French army evacuated the city after his death, headed toward Montreal.

* * *

When the British soldiers entered Quebec City, Margery looked for Captain Stobo and learned that he had missed the great battle. He had been sent to a General Amherst with messages from General Wolfe. She knew that many of the English ships would be sailing soon for England.

She talked to one of the captains. He said, "There is room for you and Janet if you . . ."

"If we leave this week!"

"This is September, and my understanding is that we are about out of food and we must sail out soon or be ice-bound and hungry in the St. Lawrence for the entire winter."

Margery stopped, gave a sigh and then broke into a smile.

"I thank you for this news. Even though we will be going to England, I feel as if Janet and I will be finally on our way home to Pennsylvania. I can't believe how happy I am to see cold weather coming. It is speeding us on our way."

Margery's face became serious, "I don't think I have enough money for passage. Does anyone know how much fare is required?"

"Captain Blaisedale, is aware of your circumstance," Henri broke in saying, "As you know, Most of our furs are still here and undamaged. Take three bundles of marten fur; sell them in England or to Captain Blaisedale if he will accept that for passage. It will be our gift to you and Janette."

Margery blinked to hold back her tears of gratitude. Quietly, she said: "Our family has been through so much pain and tribulation for so long and then the merciful God brought me to you two. Bless you. May God bless you."

* * *

In October of 1759, all hands prepared to cast off. Many men were aloft, tying down lines, and stowing the last of the passengers' belongings on the tidy ship. Margery and Janet did their best to keep out of the way. Janet was now six. She endeared herself to the crew with her quick smile and many questions about the workings of the ship.

"What do these things do?"

The seaman smiled and answered, "They are belaying pins. When the sails are just right to catch the winds, we ties them lines to the pins."

"Where are the sails? I don't see sails."

"We are in the St. Lawrence River. The current of the river, and the tide will take us to the ocean. The wind is coming at us now but it doesn't make any difference because the current of the river is strong. When the wind changes, we will unfurl the sails."

Janet thought about this for quite some time.

"You have a lot of big ropes here, I keep falling over them."

"Right," Said the seaman. "But we calls'em lines. Landlubbers calls'em ropes."

"Oohh," mused Janet. "I want to call them lines, too."

Janet was quiet for a while. Margery asked,

"What are you thinking about?"

Janet asked, "Am I a Landlubber? Is the ocean trip dangerous?"

Her mother thought about how to answer these questions.

"Yes, my little Landlubber, it could be dangerous. Even at your young age, you have seen a lot of danger. You saw Quebec City mostly destroyed by cannon balls. You saw soldiers who were horribly wounded or killed in battle. And when you were just a baby, you survived so much: Indian capture, being brought to Quebec by Baubee, the trader. You were so blessed by being able to live some years with the Duchats. God must have a good plan for you. If we have good luck, in less than a year you will be seeing your big brother Hugh and your Daddy. Yes, Janet. Life can be dangerous but we seem to be guided by a hand that protects us."

"We are on a stout ship with a good captain and crew and we will be just fine, little Lady," said the captain who had been listening to the conversation.

Just then, there was a surge of westerly winds and the captain started telling the officers to take the ship out and the nimble sailors scrambled aloft to open the sails. The creaking and lurching of the ship made it seem as though the ship had come alive. It was as if the ship said, "This is what I know how to do."

The British flotilla had been a fifty mile line of ships when they made their way up the treacherous St. Lawrence to attack Quebec. The French had not been prepared because they thought the English ships would have too much trouble making the trip. The captain laughed when he heard this.

"This river is a jolly time compared to the Thames."

The ships lined up to make the passage through the narrows and the adventure had begun.

Chapter XIII

Forbes Road

News traveled fast along the frontier. The word that several thousand troops were being assembled at the newly built Fort Ligonier for an assault on the French at Ft. Duquesne, at the Forks of the Ohio, excited the war-weary frontiersmen.

Hugh Martin and his father, John, were repairing fences around the oldest pasture. It was a clear and cold September day. Hugh stopped working, turned to his father, and said,

"I want to go. I can handle it. I'll go to Ft. Ligonier and offer myself as a Scout for that army that is going to Ft. Duquesne."

John stopped and straightened his aching back. He had been digging a new posthole in the rocky soil.

"Hugh, have you thought this through? You know how dangerous those battles can be. Look what happened to General Braddock's fine army."

"I haven't thought about anything else."

"Hugh, you are just twenty. You have a lot to learn. I may not need you here so much as winter comes on, but it is time to go on down to Philadelphia to work for those lawyers. That is a great chance to advance your education."

Hugh smiled. "That's true. It is such an opportunity in Philadelphia and I really like the work. But, I know the mountains. I know a lot of Indians. I've spent time with Indian scouts like Andrew Montour and I think I have a feel for it. I think I know how Indians think. I can handle myself in the woods as well as you can. I can track anything or anyone in the woods as well as you can. I can be of use to General Forbes."

John glared at him. "You will not go. I don't want to lose any more children."

He threw down his pick and stalked off to the house. Dinner was very quiet that night, only the occasional clink of a fork on a plate could be heard. Finally John said,

"And just when do you think that you will leave?"

"First light, tomorrow," replied Hugh. "I'll set up my pack tonight."

John answered, "If I were you, I'd lose some sleep tonight. I'd think on it."

John stood up, poked the fire a little, then strode off to bed. He did not say a good night.

Hugh had never gone against his father's wishes before. Was this a rite of passage into manhood?

"Manhood," thought Hugh. "Haven't I seen enough already?"

He remembered the massacred bodies of his Great Cove neighbors. He thought about the dead and wounded at Braddock's defeat. He remembered the dying General Braddock. He remembered trying to shield his father from the terrible realities of what had happened to the family. Sometimes he felt that he, himself, was an old man.

A cold but flaming dawn greeted Hugh as he quietly closed the door of the cabin behind him, then he melted into the nearby woods on the western hill side of the farm. Five minutes later a twig snapped. Hugh slipped behind a tree. He looked, and waited.

"Hugh," his father said. "I know that you are behind that oak tree."

John approached. "Here, Son. Take my Frazier rifle. It is a lot more accurate than your smooth bore. Keep this gun cleaned and oiled. It won't let you down. This is a loan. I will want it when you get back. If I were Bouquet, I'd hire you just because you have a rifled gun. There is a Colonel there at Ft. Ligonier that you have met, John Armstrong. He is very, very good. He's a real Pennsylvanian, better than some Virginians I could name. Find him and sign on with him. Good luck, Son."

They swapped the guns, powder, and lead and Hugh slung his pack higher and swung into a long-legged gait and soon, he was far up the hill. He turned and shouted,

"I'll be back. I promise."

John was watching as Hugh knew he would be. He waved; and Hugh waved returned his wave. John turned sadly to go down to the lonely cabin.

* * *

Hugh Martin covered the sixty miles to Fort Ligonier in four days. Col. Armstrong assigned him to a group of scouts protecting the road construction. The scouts' job was to be ten minutes ahead of the main force, with other scouts two to five minutes off each side. Young scouts, good runners, would be sent to the officers in charge with information. The scouts were not on the Forbes road, but in the forest ahead of the construction and off to the sides. They would be the first to encounter raiders and warn the road builders.

The expedition was, in comparison with other attempts to capture Ft. Duquesne, massive. It was almost 6000 men, three times the size of General Braddock's force in 1755. In addition to the "Royal Force," about 700 friendly Indians, Cherokees and Catabwas, were there. These Indian allies, however, once the six thousand pounds of gift money ran out, started deserting so that by the end of October, only eighty were left.

There was a disastrous and misguided attack on the French Fort on September 14. A Major James Grant decided on his own to launch the attack. In vain did more experienced Indian fighters like Cols. Washington, Armstrong, and Mercer try to dissuade him. Bouquet remonstrated,

"This is foolhardy. I know your tactics will be the same as those of General Braddock. You believe in a European style of engagement. The Indians and the French, who use Indian tactics, will slaughter you. I do not approve, nor would General Forbes."

The arrogant and ambitious Grant replied,

"I know I can win this battle, you will see."

Days later, early in the morning, we find Major James Grant, dressed in his best uniform, on what will be named Grant Street, not after U.S. Grant, but after this British officer, in what became Pittsburgh. The sleeping Fort was below him.

He awoke the fort with the blaring of 50 bagpipes. Hundreds of Indians and French poured out of the fort. Most of the French took off running unseen either up the Monongahela banks or up the banks of the Allegheny and soon had flanked the impetuous Grant. The small force in front of the fort lured Grant to advance even more and then the trap was sprung. Attacked from both sides, Grant's men soon found themselves in a fierce hand to hand battle. They could not handle the fighting on three sides. One third of Grant's men were killed or captured. The survivors mounted a semi-organized retreat to Ft. Ligonier. After the battle,

Chief Tecaughretango told James Smith, who was a captive in the fort, that Grant *"had made too free with spirituous liquors"* during the night and had become intoxicated about daylight.

After this battle, which afforded the Indians a great amount of scalps and loot, they went home, not expected back until the next spring.

General Forbes, who was in ill health, arrived at the newly finished Ft. Ligonier and made it his base of operation against the French and their Indian allies. He used Ligonier as a final staging point before launching an attack on Fort Duquesne.

On November 12, of 1758, Colonel George Washington was several miles away from Fort Ligonier with a scouting party. They were looking for a group of Indians with some French who had just attacked the Fort. They caught up with the raiders and engaged them. Washington's men killed one and took three prisoners.

Colonel Hugh Mercer, hearing the muskets firing, sent a party of Virginia soldiers to go to Washington's aid. It was now dusk, and in the approaching darkness, this troop saw soldiers and some Indians. Mistaking Washington's group for enemy raiders, Mercer's men commenced firing on them. Washington thought that he was under attack by another enemy group so his men returned the fire. Both units fired on their unknowing friends. Col. Washington realized the situation first and ordered a cease fire, which, under the din of musketry, was not heard by all. Washington once again proved his incredible bravery and charmed life by running in front of his men and slashing his drawn sword upward against the muskets that were fixing on each other.

Once the firing had stopped the sad results were apparent. Two officers were killed and thirty-eight privates killed or wounded in this unfortunate engagement.

The Indian captives that Washington took from the raiding party told Gen Forbes that Ft. Duquesne was at very low strength. Many Indians had gone home to help their families. They did not want to winter at Ft. Duquesne, which was poorly supplied. This information led General Forbes to march on to the Forks of the Ohio at once.

Forbes ordered Col. John Armstrong and Col. Bouquet to advance with one thousand men. Col. Washington was in advance of them with fifteen hundred men. November 17, General Forbes left Ft. Ligonier with forty-three hundred men leaving only a small garrison at Ft. Ligonier. All those forces encamped at Bushy Run, but on different days. By Nov. 24, the entire army was only twelve miles from the French fort. Indian scouts brought back a report that Ft. Duquesne was on fire. Capt. Haslet was sent with a detachment to put out the fire. At midnight, Gen. Forbes and his men "heard a dull and heavy booming sound over the western woods." The magazine at Ft. Duquesne had been blown up by the departing French soldiers.

The next morning the entire army took over the Forks of the Ohio and raised the British Flag. Four long, bloody years of war on the Pennsylvania frontier were ended. French had no more power over the Valley of the Ohio. Gen. Forbes ordered Nov. 26 as a day of Thanksgiving. In Honor of William Pitt, the Great Commoner, he named The Forks: Pittsburg.

Chapter XIV

Negotiations at Ft. Ligonier

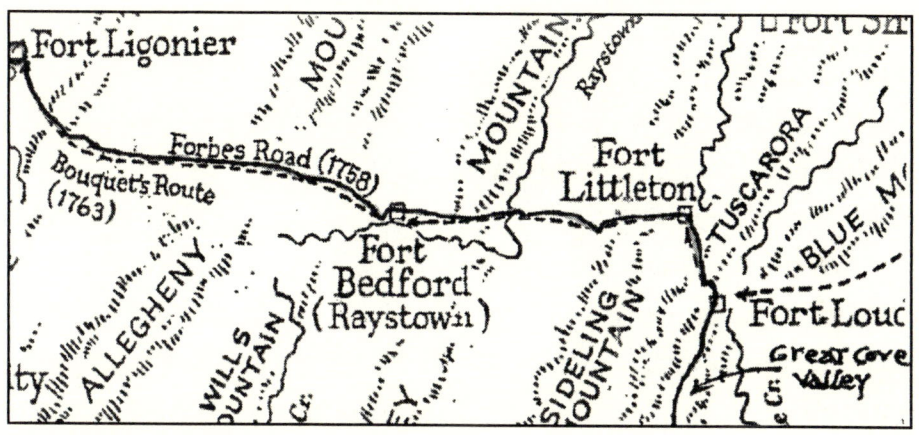

The French and Indian War ended officially in 1763 with the Treaty of Paris. It had ended locally when Fort Duquesne fell in 1758.

Fort Pitt, replacing Ft. Duquesne, was a two year building project that started in September of 1759 and was not finally completed until the summer of 1761 under Col. Bouquet. Many of the captive whites were returned by the Indians to George Croghan who was at Fort Pitt. The Delawares and Shawnees brought 388 captives to Croghan whose title was now, Indian Deputy Agent for Sir William Johnson. The Martin children were not among the returnees.

Later, John Martin heard that he might be able to talk to some of the Ohio Indians who were coming to Fort Ligonier to discuss treaties. He was already in Bedford Village, selling horses. He bought some supplies for the trip and some gifts for the Indians: tobacco and pipes. He looked forward to traveling alone through the lonely mountains. It was not as lonely there as it had been. Indeed regular supplies went through to Fort Pitt and Fort Ligonier. However, the chance of an attack by a wayward Indian or robber was an element of the trip, adding to its interest.

He had one of his smaller horses, a descendant of the beloved Nellie, called Nellie 3. She was an eager filly whose delicate hooves could usually find firm footing on the Forbes Road that had been fashioned a few years back and used continuously and therefore improved. There was the long stretch of flat land west of Bedford. It was already beginning to be farmed by the more adventurous frontiersmen. The soil looked to be less rocky than that at Great Cove and John began to think about perhaps moving west, to a more gentle valley.

He climbed the rough road that led up the Allegheny Ridge, marveling again at the tremendous effort that had been done to make that trail up the ridge. He and his Percherons had hauled not just a few rocks, stones, and logs to clear the road. It had been the hardest thing that most of the men who worked on it had ever done, and, with the ever present danger of Indian attacks. Sometimes the fellows who went into the forest were never seen again. He remembered the wagons being pulled up the mountain with winches or levered by the incredible efforts of men using logs for levers. Even his biggest Percherons could not pull the cannon up that hill. It was still a strenuous walk up the Allegheny Mountain, leading a horse.

When he reached the top, John paused to eat his rations. Then he rode carefully, listening for any sounds that might become a problem and hearing anew birds and forest sounds that he had grown used to. It was time for quiet contemplation and renewing devotions. He gave thanks for the return of his beloved Margery and little Janet. Hugh was safely in Philadelphia, studying the law. This "promised land" was, indeed, beautiful, majestic, and powerful. The sacrifices had been great but he was glad to be alive and still in good health at his advancing age. He felt that the solitary trip would be good for his soul. When he came to a small stream, he followed it for a while until he found a good camping spot, away from the road.

Forbes' men had worked fast to build the road. There had been a bit of a fuss because Forbes did not choose to go to The Forks by the road that General Braddock had built. After all, that road had gone to a spot only eight miles from Ft. Duquesne. John knew from local gossip that the Virginian, Washington, had been very upset that the Virginian road was not used. Forbes had decided that a road connecting the Forks with the great supply of food of the Eastern Pennsylvania farms was worth the expense and toil of building a totally new one. The Virginia land speculators were very annoyed. They had done much more to furnish money and troops to the war effort than had the recalcitrant Quakers. They felt they deserved what would be the spoils of the Ohio Country.

He arrived in time to see what might have been Delawares or perhaps Seneca Indians present. Fort Ligonier was large and strong and well manned. The Indians were camped a distance away, having teepees and horses.

After first making himself known to the red coated soldiers at the fort, John asked the soldier who seemed most in charge if he knew the Indians.

"Yes. They have been coming around lately, being fairly friendly. We give them what we can of our stores to try to build some sort of dealings. Do you talk Indian?"

"Well I used to be able to make myself understood. That was a while ago. They took my family: my wife and five of my children."

"I am sorry about that. Did you get any back yet?"

"Yes, my wife, she is just an incredible person. She made her way back with the youngest, a little girl. They had quite an adventure. The Indians still have two sons and a daughter. That's why I'm here. George Croghan sent word that I might be able to talk to them."

"You will have to leave any weapons here with me," said the soldier. John looked quizzically and the soldier said,

"They aren't supposed to be armed while they are here. But be careful."

John tried to assemble his thoughts and just how to approach the savages.

"Well, good luck," said the soldier and went back to his work.

John left the fort and approached the Indians, who had been watching him. They were not dressed for war. They dressed much like John in fringed buckskins. John had a simple hand made leather hat and the Indians had a few decorative feathers in their hair.

"My name is John Martin."

The Indians nodded all around, and grunted.

"Your name?" asked John.

"Me Chief Tuscarawas," answered the most imposing one. John didn't catch the others names.

He figured this one would understand best. He stood in front of the chief and looked him in the eyes and said,

"I look for sons. Two sons. One is sixteen and the other fourteen. They blonde. Like me." John tugged on his own hair which wasn't as blonde as it had been. He pointed to his eye,

"Blue. Blue like my eyes. Jimmy and Willie. They with Indian eight years. Great Cove! Martin children from Great Cove! Shingas took children, seven years ago!" He tried not to yell to help them understand. They talked together a bit and then Tuscarawas said:

"Yes. We have sons. Very good Delaware and Seneca braves. Strong. Good with axe."

John's heart pounded even more that it had. "I am very happy. Happy. Yes. I am happy."

The Indians smiled ever so slightly. They started to walk away.

"No. Don't go," John followed them further from the fort and toward what appeared to be their teepee by the creek. "You might have my daughter. Her name is Martha! She is young woman. Nineteen. Blonde hair. Blue eyes. Girl."

Tuscarawas kept walking away. John managed to get in front of the group. "Do you have my daughter?"

Tuscarawas shrugged and kept walking.

"Do you have my daughter? I want to know if you have my daughter." John was trying to keep his temper in check.

Tuscarawas kept walking toward the teepee. John said, "Please stop. Stop. Please."

The chief turned and with an angry face said, "Yes, we have daughter. Red face, red hair girl."

"Red hair? Red face?" asked John? "My daughter?"

"Girl paint face red. Paint hair red. Good squaw but strange." He shrugged his shoulders and inclined his head to indicate that the girl was hard to understand.

John felt another jolt of joy. Now he grinned widely. "That is good. That is very good. I want two sons, and daughter to come home."

The chief motioned for his pals to come close and they had a spirited discussion. The chief nodded with satisfaction and rubbing his hands together went back to John.

"We live in peace with your sons, daughter. Many years. They strong. They good. When you pay much wampum, we bring back."

John's joy took a sudden downturn. The rage that he had felt for years welled up and without thinking it through, he answered indignantly:

"I don't remember hiring you to take care of my family!"

Tuscarora looked shocked, as if John had slapped him. He reached for the tomahawk that usually hung from his belt that he would normally use to dispatch the likes of this bothersome white man. It wasn't there because of the deal with the soldiers that they would not carry weapons. He turned to two of his braves and motioned for them to grab John.

John took off running with a speed that he didn't know he possessed. The two Indians missed him and instead of chasing him on foot, started to look around for their horses. Then they went running the opposite direction for their ponies. John headed for the woods and was soon out of sight.

The custom of these Indians was to tie little bells on their horses so they could find them while they were out grazing or in the forest. John looked back and was cheered to see that running for their horses made the horses nervous and they moved away to the annoyance of the Indians.

A sentry at the fort noticed the action and shouted to someone in the fort, but John figured that by the time the soldiers could get themselves organized to help him, he would be beyond help. He ran as if he were a young fellow. He was fifty-one. The Indians, he remembered, looked to be his own age and perhaps they, too, might not be as swift as they had been in their youth.

Since he had just come down Laurel Ridge he knew that if he stayed away from the Forbes Road, he might just be able to make his way through the masses of laurel and rhododendron thickets and lose them. While dashing and zigzagging breathlessly up the mountain for what seemed like hours, he would pause to listen for the horse bells. The Indians on horseback were held up by the undergrowth and rough collections of grey, lichen covered rocks that could destroy a horse.

When John finally reached the top of the mountain and could no longer hear the breaking branches and whooping yells of the angry Indians, and the bells on their horses, he gave thanks that his life had been spared. He would miss that horse, but the first Nellie had left with Shingas a while back, and then left again with the children and Shingas. Perhaps Nellie Three was also meant to be an Indian pony. There was a wide area at the top and he was able to rest his aching body. He stopped to lie down by a creek and put his face in the fresh cool water.

* * *

Later that year, Margery and Janet Martin made their way from Liverpool, England to the harbor at New Castle on the Delaware.

"Momma, why does this ship sit out here? I have had enough sea travel. That doesn't look like as big a city as Liverpool, but I'd be glad to get off. How far are we from Great Cove? Does anyone know that we are coming? Why do we have to wait here?" Janet stamped her foot in impatience. Her petticoats were getting damp and that would be bothersome. They had a tendency to cling to her legs and make moving difficult. Margery had on her best woolen dress with the matching jacket. She sat patiently on a coil of rope hoping that the newest colony of lice would not be bothersome. Water was in short supply, crowding was suffocating, and the heat was rising. She answered patiently,

"It seems that this harbor is very full. There are many ships like ours waiting to unload. Lots of our fellow Presbyterians are coming to Pennsylvania."

It was early October of 1762. Margery and Janet had spent almost two years in England. There, as in Quebec, the irrepressible Margery had found employment to support the pair and save money for the trip to the Pennsylvania Colony. Working as a tutor in a wealthy home not only gave them security and pleasant surroundings but excellent food, the best of hand-me down clothing, and interesting folk to talk to. Janet's education proceeded rapidly and she was able to maintain her ability in French and progress in English. When they dined with their wealthy employers, Janet would cross herself as she had done for years with the Duchets; Margery hissing,

"That is superstition. The Devil isn't coming to dinner."

Margery pointed to a rowboat that seemed to be headed their way.

"Perhaps this boat is coming to tell us why we seem to be stuck out here."

The small craft approached and the ship's captain came to the gunwale to meet the two men in the rowboat.

"What say ye gentlemen? What is your news?"

The passenger stood up, waved to the captain, and said,

"Our docks are full with ships waiting. We could send out small boats so you could unload passengers."

"Do it, then. We'd be most grateful. We are about out of food."

Margery and Janet were on the first small boat, Margery having been prepared, as usual, for the next step of her life. They were helped onto the docks. Margery and Janet had given away most of their beautiful clothing. It was a sad parting but they knew that they would not need parasols and the like on the frontier and carrying useless gimcrackery would only cause them pain.

They made their way to the Presbyterian Church in hopes of finding help in traveling to the frontier. It was there. The local church had a regular system for helping the newly arrived to travel onward. Almost twelve thousand new Scotch-Irish were arriving every year and almost one-third of the residents of the colonies were Scotch-Irish. The British were glad to see that troublesome bunch leave the home islands. The Scotch did not want to recognize the King as the head of the church or pay taxes to the state church. Those Scotch had backed the Stuarts and it wasn't just Mary, the queen, who had lost a head.

At their church, the new arrivals could meet with other travelers headed west. There they could join others to make the trip more enjoyable and have the safety of numbers.

"Wir gehen zu Chambers Mills. Mein bruder ist im Chambers Mills. I'm sorry. I know I must talk English now."

Margery laughed.

"Herr Mueller, I understand Deutch. I worked for the Frantz family in Northumberland some years ago. But it is better for you to learn the English and my Janet will understand the talk better."

So it was that the Mueller family of four, Hans, Marie, and two children spent a month with Margery and Janet. Janet enjoyed teaching the Mueller children to count in English and then moved on to the times tables. The travelers would have help from the churches that would provide shelter and food when possible.

The trip got to be more fun as they went along, getting used to the creaky old wagon and shambling horse. They got tougher from walking all day and sleeping out many nights. The thrill of anticipating the reunion with Hugh and John kept their spirits up.

They parted from the Muellers at Chambers Mills and loaded with food from Hans' brother set off on foot to finish the last 25 miles, too impatient to wait for other travelers. They made the distance in two days.

Margery and Janet could see in the distance the smoke coming from the Martins' chimney. The house was on a rise just west of Great Cove Creek. As they crossed the creek, they dropped their bundles and ran, laughing and stumbling and shouting,

"We're home! We're home!"

Hugh and John, rifles in hand, ran outside to see what the commotion was about. John leaned his gun against the cabin and grabbed Hugh's arm.

"Do you see what I see or am I dreaming?"

Hugh leaned his rifle against the wall and leaned against it, too.

"I think that that is my Momma."

Janet reached them first.

"I'm Janet. I'm Janet. Daddy, Daddy." She hugged Hugh and then her dad and then went back to Hugh and back to her dad. Margery was a bit slower coming up the hill but not less enthusiastic in her greeting.

She and John hugged like a couple of trees that had grown together.

"It has been seven long years," said Margery. "I missed you every second of them."

John's tears were streaming down his face. He tried to wipe them away with the sleeve of a rough shirt.

"Margie, Margie. I have missed you so," he said and more tears poured down. "You look good."

"I'm old. I'm getting grey."

"I love you in grey. You look great," he hugged her again.

"I think Mom and Dad need some time to get reacquainted," said Hugh to Janet. "Let's go around and I'll show you the farm."

He took her parcel and tossed it in the cabin and grabbed Janet's hand and they went to look at the new barn.

"How old are you now? Nine?"

"That's right," said Janet and went skipping off with Hugh.

At the plantation, John and Hugh had rebuilt again after the cabin was burned in 1755 by Shingas. Once it was done, John had swallowed his pride and gone to George Croghan for help. A long, plain talk with the big Irish trader had reviewed their history: Croghan was one of the group who had burned the Martin cabin in 1750. Croghan said it was because he was ordered to do so by the Provincial government and John argued that Croghan wanted the settlers out because he, Croghan, wanted to own the Martins' land and wanted it for sale to newer settlers. Croghan never would admit to that and perhaps it was not true, but he came to admire John Martin's steadfast earnestness about recovering his family from the Indians. Croghan as Indian agent for Pennsylvania, had the most contact with the fearsome enemy.

Croghan had bought every Percheron that John could spare, at premier prices. He was, however, often short of cash from giving very generous gifts to the Indians to keep them calm. Times were difficult and John decided that Croghan's promises were as acceptable as anyone else's. He also hired Hugh to work at the trading post until, because Croghan had fortified it well, and then left, it was turned into Fort Shirley. Hugh was a kid who was good at sums and could write with almost legal precision. And Hugh, like his father, was of unimpeachable honesty, a sincere desire to learn, and a very hard worker. Croghan took him to Philadelphia several times to help with his dealings with the merchants and politicians there. In the winters, Hugh would spend some time clerking for lawyers in the city. Everyone was favorably impressed with the amiable, sturdy young man from the frontier.

In the years from 1758 to 1762 Christian Fredrick Post was trying to get Shingas and King Beaver to come to Philadelphia for a peace conference. They were reluctant because their actions during the war were so horrible and they feared the kind of retribution that some other Indians had suffered on what was supposed to be a peaceful trip to the "City of Brotherly Love."

1759 June to 1761 George Croghan, having given up the trading business was deputy Indian Agent to Sir William Johnson. The three hundred thirty-eight captives, released from the Indians, at Fort Pitt and many at Carlisle in that period. The Martin children and the Knox family were not among them. In 1761 John and Hugh had spent time in Croghan Hall, that busy man's newest home at the mouth of Pine Creek near Fort Pitt. They were able to gather information about the people who had been taken prisoner by Shingas. John was fairly sure that his children were still alive. He understood that many of the captives were far into the Ohio country.

Chapter XV

John's Trip to the Muskingum

It was some time after his unfortunate encounter with the chiefs at Fort Ligonier that John was given a chance to go with some traders and a load of trade goods to Chief Shingas' camp at Coshockton in the Ohio country. He went with the excuse of carrying messages to the Indians.

Dressed like a trader, John was able to ride one of his own sturdy Percherons. He carried a rifle, his hunting knife, and almost a month's supply of food. His experience with the pack train was a memory that he enjoyed telling grandchildren about in his later years. The pack train moved at a pace that John could not have believed. The horses and mules needed no urging to move as if they had a serious mission to perform. They didn't stop to browse, but kept up a strong, intense pace through each day and then were ready to go again the next day. John would stretch himself out and urge the Percheron to unusual speeds. His horse seemed to enjoy the challenge and was soon able to find a pace that kept up with the other horses and mules. John had joined the pack train as it wound its way to Fort Bedford, then, following the Forbes Trail, up the perilous climbs over Allegheny Mountain and down from the Laurel Ridge Mountain on the trail that John remembered well from his previous trip to Fort Ligonier.

The trail moved on by the Loyalhanna stream that had cut a gorge through Chestnut Ridge into the softly rolling hills beyond. John stopped several times to imagine having a farm in one of these pleasant valleys. He later told his son, Hugh, about these peaceful glens in the foothills, west, beyond the Chestnut Ridge.

There were small trading posts along the way where a trader would have a store of hay and oats for the animals and even extra animals to replace those that had become too tired to continue. The trail continued down Turtle Creek past the battlefield where so many British soldiers under General Braddock had died. Only recently had provincial soldiers found the bones and given them a Christian burial. At Fort Pitt there was a rest period to refresh and change some animals. Then the pack train was off at its astonishing pace. John had been given messages to deliver to Shingas from Colonel Bouquet and Governor Morris.

In a day's breakneck pace, they passed through Logstown, situated seventeen miles and an half, fifty-seven perches, by the path from Fort Pitt. This place was noted before the French and Indian war for the great trade carried on there by the English and later, French; but its inhabitants, the Shawnees and Delawares, abandoned it in the year 1758. The lower Logstown had extended about sixty perches over a rich bottom to the foot of a low steep ridge, on the summit of which, near the declivity, stood the upper town, commanding a most agreeable aspect over the lower and quite a view across the Ohio, which is about five hundred yards here, and by its majestic, easy current added much to the beauty of the place.

Proceeding beyond Logstown, through a fine country, interspersed with hills and rich valleys, watered by many rivulets, and covered with stately timber. There was on a level piece of ground, with a thicket in the rear, a small precipice in the front, with a run of water at the foot, and good graze for the horses. This days run was without many hills.

At about three miles distance from this former camp, they came again to the Ohio, pursuing its course a half mile farther, and then turning off, over a ridge they crossed Big Beavercreek, which was twenty perches wide, the ford stony and pretty deep. It runs through a rich vale, with a pretty strong current, its banks high, the upland joining it. The timber was tall and young. About a mile below its confluence with the Ohio, stood formerly a large town, this had been the home of King Beaver, on a steep bank, built by the French of square logs, with stone chimneys, for some Shawnees, Delawares, and Mingo tribes, who abandoned it in the year 1758, when the French deserted Fort Du Quesne. Near the fording of Beavercreek also had stood about seven houses, which were deserted by the Indians who had destroyed the houses themselves when they went further west.

Then crossing the Little Beaver and Yellow Creek they advanced as far as the forks of the Muskingum.

John Martin arrived with a traders' pack train at the Indian village of Tuscarawas. Here were broad fields of corn and at least 400 cabins with smoky fires for cooking nearby. The usual dogs and chickens announced their entrance into the village and the Indians came running from everywhere to wonder at what the traders had brought. The traders approached the chief's cabin. They waited patiently for the head man to greet them and, in what seems to be a universal ritual: get his palm greased with gifts. The Indians were overjoyed to have the traders come and prepared a feast.

John looked at every young brave to see if any looked like Jimmy or Willie. He looked for the girl with a red face and red hair. He was, nervously, on the lookout for Tuscarawas also. John helped to care for the horses and tried not to attract attention. He was given a place to stay with the other traders and invited to the feast. He decided to skip that.

Then Shingas came out, short, dark skinned, scars of a dozen battles on his body; ugly, but dominating. Shingas was followed by three Indian lads who were young versions of Shingas. Shingas' sons. After a bit of watching John decided that Shingas was the head Chief, and that Shingas lived in the big cabin in the center of the camp. He watched two young braves come out of the cabin and his heart skipped a beat.

It had to be Jimmy and Willie. They were so handsome! They were perfect. Tall, strong, lithe. They moved with the grace of . . . Indians. His sons! They each had a blonde top knot decorated with feathers. His throat choked up with pride.

The squaws were next. One of them was a girl with red face and red hair. She was no beauty, but she must be Martha. Another girl held her hand. The other girl was painted also with an ochre face and ochre hair. She was also pretty unattractive.

John rose and started toward his children. Tuscarawas appeared from nowhere and said something to Shingas. He pointed at John.

Shingas turned toward John and got between him and his children. Realizing that this was going to require more than his usual tact, John chose his words with care.

"Chief Shingas? I am John Martin. I have met you before the war. We used to trade furs. We smoked at my home." John offered his hand.

Shingas folded his arms over his chest and did not take the proffered hand. "Me Shingas. Chief of the Delaware."

He tilted his head to glare up at John who must have been at least a head taller. Then he relaxed and decided to invite John to the feast. The two went into the cabin and settled down for a typical Indian feast and parlay. They were joined by many chiefs and some of the traders. John's stern Presbyterian upbringing did not permit much alcohol. However, Shingas enjoyed drinking the newly arrived rum so they didn't have much to talk about as Shingas and the other Delawares and the traders indulged in the drink that both the Quakers and the Indians had tried to ban from the Indians. Sometimes the Indians used to go to the Quakers and complain that their children were being ruined by rum.

When offered rum by the Chief, John would smell it and then wave his finger and roll his eyes up to indicate drunkenness. At this Shingas laughed. When Shingas laughed the rest of the Indians and then the traders joined in. Tuscarawas showed up but expressed no hostility. Anyhow, that put enough of a damper on the drinking that they didn't get completely unconscious or dangerous.

John did manage to get some concessions from Shingas. First, the two boys that he had seen were, indeed, Jimmy and Willie. Shingas protested that they had been treated as his own children, lived in this cabin with his family. He felt as though he had been their father. He would think about returning them to John. But not now. They were needed here now. About Martha, she was, indeed, the strange looking girl with the red face and red hair. Not just red, but vermillion. She peeked around from the other end of the cabin at John but did not risk talking to him.

Finally, John got out the letters to Shingas and King Beaver from Col. Bouquet, Governor Morris, and George Croghan that he was carrying and helped make sure that Shingas understood them.

The letters named Martha Martin and asked for her release.

Shingas still refused to let Martha go. He would not make the slightest concession. She would stay and the other strange, ochre girl would stay also. The thought of leaving the girls with these savages was chilling but there wasn't much John could do. He buried his anger and politely thanked Shingas for his courtesy. He knew that Shingas and King Beaver were afraid that they would have to answer for the horrible crimes against the settlers. The Indians had released many prisoners in August of 1762 to the Lancaster Council, but John could see many white people still here in the camp who were obviously captives.

He gave soft answers to the chief and left the village when the traders started back. The traders had some furs to take away but were in general the loads were much lighter. They were even faster on the return trip. They were soon back in Pennsylvania.

At Fort Pitt, John stopped to talk to Col. Bouquet and report on the whites still in captivity at the Ohio camp. The Colonel turned red with rage at the stubbornness of Chief Shingas.

John made a detour to Croghan Hall to report to George Croghan also. That busy man was away on a trip to London, England trying to establish his right to Ohio lands.

When John arrived home, he got his eldest son, Hugh, and the two sat down to write a letter to Governor James Hamilton at the Lancaster council:

August 1762

> *The humble petition of your most Obedient Servant Sheweth, Sir, may it pleas Your Excellancy, Hearing me in your clemacy a few words. I one of the bereaved of my wife and five children, by Savage War at the captivity of the Great Cove, after many and Long Journeys, I lately went to Indian Town, viz, Tuskaroways 150 miles beyond Fort Pitts, and entreated on in Co. Bocquits and Co. Croghan's favor So as to bear their letters to King Beaver and Shingas, Desiring them to Give up one of my daughters to me. Whiles I have yet two sons and one other daughter, if alive, among them-and after Seeing my daughter with Shingas he refused to give her up, and after some Expostulating with him, but all in Vain, he promised to Deliver her up with the other Captive to Yr Excellencies Beneficent influence in favor of Yr Excellencies Most Obedient and Dutiful Serv't.*
>
> *John Martin*

In the spring of 1763, Chief Pontiac's forces entered Western Pennsylvania.

August 17 of 1763, one of John's neighbors was sending in the notices of the area to the Provincial Council. He mentioned that

> "one John Martin, in the Great Cove, seeing an Indian come up to a house where he was, fired at him, upon which the Indian reised a yell and took a tree; That Martin, imagining there might be more Indians near him, ran to a company at work and told what had happened, when they went to the place, found some blood and excrements, from which they concluded that he was shot through the bowels. They followed his track down to a bottom, where they saw the tracks of six or seven more, but, being a small party, pursued no farther."

In December of 1763 Col. Bouquet was in Philadelphia getting supplies for Fort Pitt when he heard about the new attacks from Pontiac. He was able to get the help from General Jeffrey Amherst. Amherst sent two companies of the 42nd Black Watch Highlanders and 77th Montgomery's Highlanders, 214 officers and men. Later, with worsening news, Amherst sent an additional 133 men from those companies.

Chapter XVI

The Battle of Bushy Run

(Fotos by Charles Martin on the front and back covers are from Reenactment at Bushy Run Battle Field August 5, 2007)

In October of 1763, matters moved very quickly in the Martins' favor. Col. Bouquet had become very angry when John stopped on the way back to Great Cove to tell him that Shingas and King Beaver were ignoring his messages, and grumbling to himself, Bouquet sent messages in every direction ordering militia to report to him. It soon became apparent that the situation was worse than just Shingas

Forts Ligonier, Bedford, and Pitt were being besieged by Guyasuta and Shingas. And also, forts all over the western side of the Alleghenies had been attacked, all the way from Maine down to the Carolinas. Half of the frontier settlers living nearby had again been slaughtered or had fled to the more eastern forts in this most organized Indian war, Pontiac's War.

General Amherst responded to Bouquet's request with two units of Highlanders Black Watch. When Bouquet, who had joined the troops at Philadelphia, arrived at Shippensburg, he was greeted by almost fourteen hundred terrified and starving refugees.

After passing Fort Loudon near Cove Mountain, the small army came to the abandoned Fort Littleton and the post at Juniata Crossing, those two having been deemed indefensible.

On July 25, 1763, Bouquet marched into Fort Bedford. The Colonel remained for three days to rest his men and horses. Here, also, thirty local frontiersmen, joined his forces. Bouquet was given the gristly details of the scourge of fire and death which had so recently swept through the mountain valleys. There had not been any news from Fort Pitt for several weeks. Every messenger had been killed. John and the family had moved back to York, fearing the renewed raids.

July 28 Bouquet left for Fort Ligonier, using Forbes Road.

On August 2, the General arrived Fort Ligonier. The Indians who had been attacking the fort fled. Still no word had come from Fort Pitt. Bouquet decided to leave the cattle that he had brought and move forward with 350 pack horses and a few cattle. The pack horses carried the flour.

On August 4, Bouquet resumed the march.

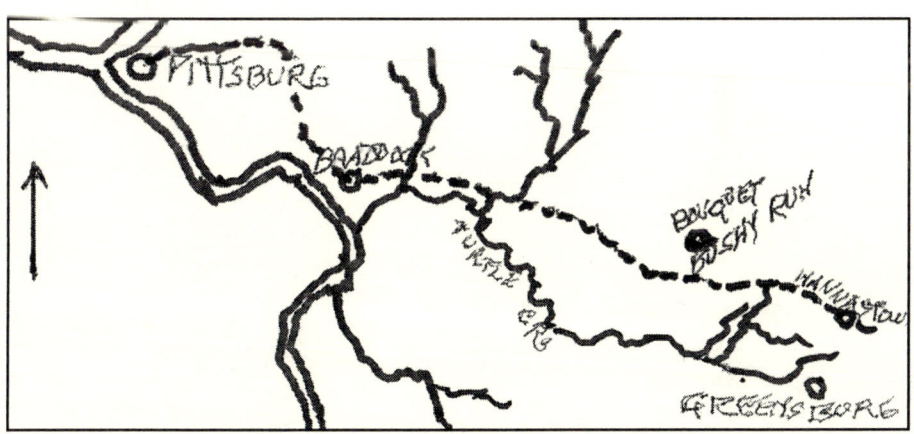

August 5 A local woodsman named Byerly led the army on an Indian path away from the Forbes Road toward Byerly's Station. They had marched seventeen miles and were just one-half mile From Byerly's Station. Suddenly the sharp report

of rifles was heard in the front, sending an energizing thrill along the ranks. The fire quickened, and the blood-curdling war whoops of hundreds of Indians rang through the shadowy forest. The decisive battle of Bushy Run was now on. The two foremost companies were sent forward to support the advance. The fire grew stronger and more raging. Bouquet knew that this was a very large force of Indians against him. A general charge made with fixed bayonets to protect the convoy of horses and supplies. The assailants were driven from the hill in front. They recovered quickly and they attacked the flanks and rear. The army found it was necessary to fall back to protect the rear and the convoy.

Colonel Bouquet was forced to take a position on a hill to the right of the road. Here the troops formed a circle around the terrified horses, and formed a barricade of flour sacks to protect the wounded and the convoy.

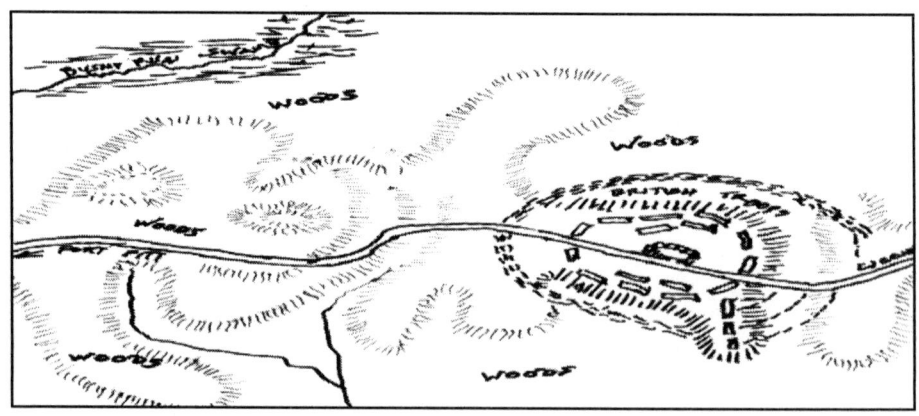

Time after time the savages rushed up with frightful yells, and endeavored to break through the barricade. They were turned back each time. The troops expanded the circle and charged into the forest. However, no sooner had the Indians been driven from one point, than they appeared at another. Their attacks continued with unabated fury. Protected by the trees and brush of the forest which fringed the hilltop, they suffered little; but Bouquet's brave troops suffered many injuries. Thus the battle went on during the remainder of the day until night settled down over the forest. The little army had by this time lost sixty in killed and wounded. It was impossible for Colonel Bouquet to change his ground in the presence of so powerful an enemy. Fearing a night attack, he posted his sentinels.

Morning arrived with the Indians' renewed war whoops. Then they fired on Bouquet's men from every side, using their rifles from trees and bushes. They tried to break through the barricade of flour sacks around the troops and convoy. The savages were driven back many times by the troops who made the circle larger and who attacked the Indians with fixed bayonets and chased them into the forest. Some of the horses, maddened by the frightful activity, escaped into the forest.

The Indians became more and more confident of victory as Bouquet's troops, although tired, still maintained an unbroken ring around the wounded and the convoy. It was now about ten o'clock. Many of Bouquet's men had fallen since the renewal of battle, without his being able to inflict any telling injury on the enemy. The commander then thought up a plan to bring a large part of the Indians together and so deliver them a telling blow.

Later Col. Bouquet sat down to write out his report:

> ". . . it was thought proper to entice them to come close upon us . . . With this in view, two companies of light infantry were ordered within the circle and the troops on their left and right opened their files and filled up the space so that it might seem that they were intended to cover the retreat. The Third Light Infantry Company and the Grenadiers of the 42nd were ordered to support the first two companies.
>
> This maneuver succeeded to our wish, for the few troops who took possession of the ground lately occupied by the two Light Infantry companies being brought nearer to the center of the circle, the barbarians mistaking these motions for a retreat, hurried headlong on, and advancing upon us, with the most daring intrepidity, galled us excessively with their heavy fire; but at that very moment that they felt certain of success, and thought themselves master of the camp, Major Campbell, at the head of the first companies, sallied out from a part of the hill they could not observe, and fell upon their right flank.
>
> They resolutely returned the fire but could not stand the irresistible shock of our men, who, rushing in among them, and put the rest to flight. The orders sent to the other two companies were delivered so timely by Captain Bassett, and executed with such celerity and spirit, that the routed savages who happened at that moment to run before their front, received the full fire

when uncovered by the trees. The four companies did not give them time to load a second time, or even to look behind, but pursued them until they were totally dispersed. The left of the savages, which had not been attacked, were kept in awe by the remains of our troops, posted on the brow of the hill for that purpose; nor durst they attempt to support or assist their right, but being witness to their defeat, followed their example and fled."

The Indians continued to make sporadic attacks but when Bouquet got to Fort Pitt, they had given up the siege and gone.

Chapter XVII

The March into Indian Country

"Rubbish!" exclaimed Colonel Bouquet.

It was September at Fort Pitt. The courier from Colonel Bradstreet, bringing a message to Col. Bouquet, had just left. The message from Bradstreet was that he had successfully negotiated a peace with the Shawnees and Delawares.

"Rubbish," exclaimed Bouquet again. "Those Indians are still raiding the frontier. They are at it, even after the date of Bradstreet's letter!"

Bouquet looked up from Bradstreet's message as his adjutant entered.

"Sir," said the soldier, there is a John Martin here who has recently been to Muskingum. He wants to tell you about his three children still held by the savages."

"Oh, yes. I know him. He is a persistent fellow; dedicated to getting his children back. He took a message out to Shingas for me. He is probably lucky to still have his hair. Show him in. I need his report about the Indian enclave."

John entered, holding his hat in hand and wondering if he should salute the Colonel. Finally, his admiration for the Colonel overcoming reticence, he saluted smartly.

"Sir, I thank you for seeing me."

John had grown a beard during his trek to the Indian village and his face was a leathery brown from his travel to the camp, some 150 miles west of Fort Pitt.

John said, "I delivered your message and the one from the Governor to Shingas. I think I was able to make him understand the messages, particularly the ones relating to my children . . ."

He was interrupted by the adjutant who entered again.

"Colonel, sorry to interrupt but there are three Indian Chiefs to see you."

"Do you know anything about this, Martin?"

"John shook his head, "No, Sir. I do not."

"Give them something to eat. I'll talk to them later. I want to hear what John Martin has to say about the camp at Muskingum."

John decided that this was one British soldier who knew how to deal with the Indians. He answered all of Colonel Bouquet's questions about Shingas' attitude, the lay of the land around the settlement, and the apparent number of warriors that John could discern from his observations.

"Mr. Martin, you have been a great help with your information. I intend to make a move very soon to release your children. You say that there may be as many as 200 other white captives?"

He rose to shake John's hand.

"Mr. Martin, I will send couriers out to the frontier towns as soon as possible to alert those relatives that more captives, like yours, will be coming home."

John left the fort confidently, feeling that good results were in the offing.

When John had gone and the Colonel had enjoyed his own lunch, he summoned the adjutant,

"Send in those chiefs now."

The message from the chiefs was that Bouquet should not send a military force into Ohio now. It was too late in the year. Waiting until spring would give more time for conferences.

Bouquet knew that the chiefs would want gifts at the conferences. Unfortunately, the new commander of the British forces, Amherst, did not have more money for gifts and had declared the practice over. There would be no more gifts for the Indians. Amherst did suggest giving a gift of small pox infested blankets to the Indians. That the unfortunate gift circumstance weakened Bouquet's hand is certainly true, but he let the blanket suggestion fade from his mind. He listened to the chiefs and then decided to present a tough face to the negotiators.

Bouquet stood up, looked each chief in the eyes, slowly. He was a stocky man, born in Switzerland, scholarly. He could speak and write German, and French, and the English writing of his reports was better than that written by most English generals. His Royal American uniform was spic and span.

"Hear me well," he said. "One of you will go back and tell your warriors that I intend to march into Ohio within the week. Chief Pipe and Captain John I will keep as hostages. You," he indicated the third chief, "will tell the Delawares and Shawnees that we are coming. Also I sent two messengers to Col. Bradstreet at Presque Isle. If these two messengers are harmed, Chief Pipe and Captain John will be executed."

The assigned messenger chief backed out of Bouquet's office and in one flowing motion slid down to his canoe and paddled briskly down the Ohio. He was soon out of sight. Bouquet ordered two soldiers who were standing guard to take the two hostage chiefs to the guard house, treat them well, but keep them under constant surveillance.

At this point, Bouquet felt that he was ready. The Virginia Colony had sent him more troops, bringing his available men count to 1500. He began his march to the Ohio Country on October 4, 1764. Two weeks later they were nearing the Indian camp. They met with the chiefs at an area near the camp.

News of Bouquet's arrival created fear among the tribes. They well knew that Bouquet had defeated the Shawnees, Delawares, Wyandots, Monimons, Miamies, and Ottawas and Mingos at Bushy Run and they had fled from the siege of Fort Pitt as he approached. Now he was almost to their camp. The Chiefs appeared to talk to Bouquet. The message was that all the chiefs would convene at a place only eight miles away. Bouquet agreed to meet them the next morning.

As soon as the Indians left, Bouquet called his adjutant, "Tell all our officers that we march tomorrow. All are to be in battle dress with arms at the ready."

When the chiefs arrived for the parlay the soldiers split into two columns: one marching around the Indians to the left, the other to the right. When the encirclement was done, there were 1500 soldiers, standing 5 feet apart, armed and making a very obvious show of strength.

The chiefs became very friendly,

"Sit down with us, please, the good Colonel Bouquet. Sit down with us. We will talk."

Bouquet could identify Delawares, Shawnees, and Mingos among the chiefs. He opened the "negotiations" by reminding them of the cruelty and barbarity of their raids, going back to those of October and November of 1755 in the Great Cove, nine years before. He told them that if they did not return the captives, he would destroy their villages and many Indian lives would be lost.

"I have brought with me relatives of the people you have massacred and those you have taken prisoner. They hunger for revenge!"

Bouquet had a powerful message and he spoke as a conqueror, having given the Indians a strong show of military presence.

Meanwhile, back at the Indian camp, the Shawnee warriors became fearful that Bouquet meant to destroy their tribe. They decided to gather all of the prisoners, kill them, and flee to Mississippi.

The Shawnees gathered the prisoners together but disaster was prevented when a messenger arrived from a horrified Bouquet saying that the Shawnees would get the same peace terms as the Delawares. Matters relaxed for a while.

Shortly after that, a British soldier was killed and the Shawnee warriors thought that they would be blamed for that. They gathered the frightened captives together again and their Mississippi plan arose again.

The Martin children, James, Martha, and William still huddled together with Susan Knox and her children. The two older girls were the most frightened. Braves that they had known for years were hitting them and threatening them with tomahawks.

"What is happening?" asked Martha of Willie and James. They were strong young braves and were usually included when the men went on hunting parties. They did not understand being herded in with the women. The white women.

"I don't know," said James. "It doesn't look good."

"Why are they pushing us around and hitting us? I thought that we were accepted into their families."

"I think that our people have finally come to save us," said Susan. I heard that there is an army just over that hill. A real army."

"It might be that they don't want us to tell about how things are here."

"Would they kill us all?" asked Willie. "Even me?"

Susan patted Willie's shoulder but he squirmed away from her motherly touch.

Meanwhile, Bouquet, had been informed that the soldier's death could cause untold trouble for the white captives. He made the correct decision.

"Send a message immediately to the Shawnee that they will not be blamed for the death of the soldier."

The message arrived in time to prevent one more massacre.

Chapter XVIII

Jane and Hugh

On November 29, 1764, Martha, James, and William Martin, along with the Knox children, Jane, Susanna, Robert, Mary, and their mother, Susan were delivered by the Indians to Fort Pitt. There were a number of others plus some Indians squaws who were lamenting the loss of their adopted children.

Jane and Martha whispered to each other and held hands tightly. It had been a long time since they had seen so many whites and they were fearful.

"What are we going to do now? What if we don't get to stay together? What will we do?" worried Martha.

"I am going to take a bath and get rid of this paint," said Jane. "Oh, look at that tall fellow. I really like how he looks."

"Which one?" queried Martha. "They all look good to me." "But do you see how they look at us? They act as if we are very strange. Ha, ha. It is the paint, isn't it? I'd like to think the paint is as offending to them as it is to the braves."

"The one over there with the big horse. He has such nice blonde hair."

"That's Hugh! That's my brother Hugh! I just know it is! There is my dad! Daddy!" Martha broke away from the crowd of returnees and ran to John Martin. They hugged and cried and rivers of tears came down Martha's cheeks, making the paint run. Her brother Hugh was standing next to John and got the second smeary hug.

"We are so glad to see you. How long you have been away!"

How strange it all was. Some people signed the roster for their relatives and left immediately. The group with John and Hugh Martin had decided to travel together for protection and dallied for a couple of days. John ended up signing for a John McCullough who had no one to meet him. As it turned out John McCullough's family had given up all hope that he would ever return home. His father had gone to Ohio, paid a sum for his son and tried to bring John back from the Indians. John had been very young when he was kidnapped. He had forgotten any English he knew and had felt that his Indian family was his own. When his real father came for him, bought him from the Indians, and started back with him, John escaped and went back to the Indians. His father had given up in disgust.

The returnees were given the use of the fort's bathing facilities and most had new clothes to wear that had been brought by their families. Hugh noticed that the Knox family had not been met by anyone and no one had brought new clothes so he asked the mother, Susan, if he could take Barbara and young Susan and her strange looking sister, Jane, into the trader's shack near the fort. He made himself very popular by buying them some new clothes. Jane, the spooky one thanked him sweetly and slid her hand into his.

Hugh took her hand and patted it. "You are very welcome. How long were you with the Indians?" he asked.

She smiled up at him and said, "Are you married? Usually I would let Martha find things out for me but I think I had better find out now if you are married. Are you married?" She cocked her head and the black pout that she had drawn for a mouth turned lopsided.

Hugh laughed. "No, are you?"

"What brave would marry a thing that looks like me? Would you marry a girl that looks like me, even if I had a beautiful calico dress like this one?" She held the dress by the shoulders to show it off.

"I might," answered Hugh. "But you'd have to be pretty rich. Are you rich?"

"Well, I have a new dress. That makes me feel very rich. Maybe I'm too rich to be interested in a frontiersman," Jane said. "I am really high society, masquerading as a clown."

She tried to flounce the dress without letting it touch her well-worn, filthy garments.

"Actually, I must be off to the baths to take my first bath in a very long time. Ta, ta."

Hugh smiled at the girl and watched her as she walked away. Martha had been to the bath area and now appeared: transformed. Her hair was the Martin blonde with just a trace of the vermillion adding sparkle. She was a woman, not a child as she had appeared.

"That is a change. I would not have believed that you could look this good. You look wonderful. Why did you use all that paint? It wasn't very attractive."

"My friend Jane and I thought it would keep the braves from looking at us. It worked very well. If only Mary had painted herself. Do you know what happened to Mary? It was so awful,"

Martha's eyes brimmed up with tears and she started to cry and then hung on to Hugh and cried as if she would never stop blurting out the awfulness of her miserable years:

"Mary is dead. She died that first year. Mama wouldn't let us cry. She said it would make us look weak. Then baby Janet got sold to a French trader and he took her away. And then Mama went to try to find Janet, and left me. Oh, Hugh, it has been so terrible. And then Jimmy and Willie went with another tribe and I haven't seen them for a long time. And Jimmy and Willie are strange, Hugh. They are just like Indians, you can't trust them. Tell Daddy that he can't trust them. They are just like Indians."

They sat together for a long time while Hugh told her about Margery and Janet's travels Martha calmed down and became much happier to learn that her mother and little Janet were alive and well and back home. Then Martha spotted Jane coming across the open area.

"Here comes my good friend, Jane. She thinks that you are the choice of the lot here. She thinks that you are very handsome," said Martha, wiping away the tears. "You be nice to Jane, please? Are you married? Jane will want to know."

"She already asked me," answered Hugh, laughing. "She isn't the shyest girl I've met."

"If she sets her cap for you, you are a gonner," Martha whispered to her brother. "At twenty years old, she is almost an old maid. So am I. I'm a year older."

"Maybe I already am a gonner," answered Hugh in a whisper. "That bath has really made a difference for her, too. I bought her that dress."

"You did? She is a fast worker."

"Nobody was here to meet the Knox family. The mother and the other three kids will probably go back to Fort Bedford with us. They seem like a good family."

"Yes, they are. I want to talk to Daddy. Where is he?"

"He and Jimmy and Willy are making a bigger camp so we can take an extra boy and the Knox family."

The strangeness for the returnees was not enough to keep the evening's fire and dinner from being a great party, with tears and hugs and amazement. Susan Knox stood and said that it was time to thank the Lord for their deliverance. She led prayers for the group as she had done in the Indian camp, but there everything had to be done secretly. She had replaced Margery as teacher when Margery left. However, the children of the Martins and the Knoxes could not read or write. They had been able to read when captured but had lost the ability. Susan had taught them all the bible verses that her prodigious memory had stored and all of the many hymns she remembered.

Jane and Hugh became inseparable on the trip back. When Hugh was driving the Percherons to pull the big Conestoga wagon with the two families bumping along inside, Jane was sitting beside him, learning how to drive the horses. When John was driving the wagon, Hugh and Jane walked behind with their heads together, talking and laughing.

Jane would say, "I don't remember ever laughing before I met Hugh."

"I'm trying to see that as a compliment," Hugh would answer, "But if you want a big laugh, ask Martha to put on the paint she wore in the Indians' camp."

This is not to say that the Martin men did not carry their guns at the ready. They had Jimmy and Willie also and those two would scout ahead and behind to make sure that there were no hostiles around. John had made a big expenditure and bought each of them a musket and shot and powder and at every stop, they and Hugh and John would practice with the guns.

"I have heard that the way to learn how to shoot is to learn to run at full speed through the forest and load and shoot and load and shoot at a dead run," said John. "I, personally, have never tried it for fear I'd hurt myself." The men all laughed, except for Jimmy and Willie.

"Me, Seneca. Me show slow, stupid white man," said Willie. He took off running through the forest, loading his musket and firing at helpless trees. Jimmy laughed and said,

"Him slow, little man. Baby. Me, big Delaware. Show little Indian." He set off zigzagging through the trees loading and shooting. Hugh and John stood amazed, shaking their heads. Later, as John was walking beside the wagon with Jimmy, the young man stopped and took an arrow from his quiver and prepared to shoot.

"What is it?" whispered John.

"A deer," answered Jimmy. A deer bounded out of the bushes and stared at the wagon, as if astonished. Jimmy's arrow went to its mark and the party had fresh meat for dinner that night.

"I never would have seen that deer," said John, later. "How did you know it was there?"

"I smelled it," answered Jimmy smiling patiently.

"How did we ever win?" said John, "It must be that the God who brought us to this beautiful, fertile land did it for a purpose. We are his people. He will give us tribulation but He will reward those who honor Him. Thank you, God for giving back to me these beautiful sons."

Later he sat Jimmy and Willie down and asked them, "Did you ever see an Indian make a bow and arrow?" They nodded.

"Of course. We make bows and arrows."

"Did you ever see an Indian make a gun?"

They shook their heads and shrugged.

"I have a friend who makes guns," said John. "He is a white man. Did you ever see an Indian make a bullet?"

They shrugged again. "White men make bullets. You have seen the squaws make bullets. Where do they get the lead?"

More shrugs.

"Do you know where gun powder comes from?"

"From the Trader," answered Jimmy. "Just like the guns and bullets. But I don't know where he gets it."

"It is a white man thing, nitre, charcoal, and sulfur." said John. "You may see Indians use guns that they bought from the traders but they don't know how to make or even repair them. That is why the whites will prevail. And then, there are more of us all the time and fewer Indians. We will prevail."

The two boys looked at each other. Any thought of arguing against this new father's logic began to fade. They began to gain respect for the graying farmer.

At that night's camp fire, each of the young former captives was asked to tell a story about their time in captivity. Jane waited until the rest were done, telling about the work, the hunger, the things they had learned about primitive living. None of them told of the horrors they had been witness to. They did not speak of the terrible tortures and bloody killings they had been forced to look at.

"My first day in camp at Kittanning," Jane began, "after the running of the gauntlet, I was given to a brave who was really mad that he had been given a worthless little girl. I was to replace his brother who had been a mighty warrior. Momma and the rest of the family were tied up and he took me to a big tree and tied me to it. Then he called me all sorts of awful things and started throwing his axe at me. Let me tell you, when that axe took a piece of my hair and buried it with the axe in the tree, I knew I was going to be dead very soon. I didn't cry because Mrs. Martin said that we had to be brave and not cry. I didn't but my family did."

"Oh. Goodness. Do you have to tell this? I was out of my mind with fear," said her mother, Susan Knox. "I prayed so loudly that I think God must have been able to hear me, away up there." Susan clasped her hands and bowed her head.

"Well, the Indians heard her and beat her terribly," said Jane. "I started to cry because they were hurting Momma. Then Robby and Susie and Mary started to cry and the Indians were sort of distracted with so many to beat. Then old Shawga, the oldest Delaware squaw, jumped into it and claimed me as a child to adopt. The tomahawk throwing brave walked away. He was really angry. He knew he had to honor the old woman's intervention. I was with her until she died a month or so later. Then Martha and I got to be friends and when Mary died we started to wear paint. You know, I probably wouldn't be here if my family wasn't so good at screaming and hollering."

"What happened to the brave? Was he a problem?" asked Hugh, he wanted to hug the young woman and reassure her that she was safe.

"He was killed by another Indian a week or so later. He was hunting with his friend and the other Indian thought he was a deer."

Everyone laughed a rueful laugh and nodded because that was a familiar story, the settlers also managed to kill each other while hunting.

"Well, let us give thanks that we are here and well," said Jane's mother. "We must believe that the merciful God has chosen us to be his people. He has brought us to this beautiful land. And we pray that He will not beset us with Indians any more. We have shown that we are strong." Susan prayed holding two of her children tightly.

"We will put this out of our minds. We will waken each day with gratitude for the day that our Lord has given us. We will give thanks to God for our freedom, and we will put this out of our minds. We will not speak of it again."

Everyone around the fire nodded in agreement and they all vowed to do their best to put the anger and hatred out of their heads and hearts and live in God's grace.

In a few days the Martin and Knox caravan arrived at the grassy glen next to Fort Ligonier.

The sun was making a spectacular splash of peach and rose on the western sky. There were several shelters there already and a brisk bustle of the preparation for the evening meal.

"I'll go check with the soldiers here and tell them who we are," said Hugh.

"I'll go along and help," chimed in Jane.

"Susan," said John to the Knox children's mother, "Have you heard from your husband?"

"No. I guess he must think that we are dead. I hope to find him in our cabin that was near Fort Bedford. I think that he might be dead. It has been nine years since we were captured."

"I met a William Knox. He has a small cabin near here. If you would like, I will take you there."

"Would that be my William? Does he know we are here? Why didn't he come to meet us?" Susan looked down. Then she shook her head. "He may not want us back. He will think that living with savages has made us savages. William has a very narrow view of right and wrong. This may be the saddest day of all for me."

Susan leaned her head toward John and whispered, "He may think that I have sinned with an Indian."

John nodded and responded, "That is how some people talk. It is ugly and terrible. I guess you are prepared for what his attitude may be."

"I don't want him to be ashamed of his family."

"We don't know how it is with him. He may be very sensible."

"He can be very hard."

* * *

In the short time since they had met, Hugh began to realize he did not want to have to part from Jane and perhaps never see her again. He was careful to give this news to his father.

"I think that I am going to stay here with the Knox family for a while. I was talking to Mr. Knox and he needs help right now. He has a couple of plantations near here and needs someone to supervise.

John shook his head slightly and said, "We need help too. And your family will miss you. What are you thinking?"

"Well, Dad, to be honest, I think that Jane is the one for me. We are making plans."

"Good. Good. It's about time you settled down. She seems like a sensible girl and she certainly likes you. She had been through a lot but she is a very strong person. She is a good choice. I am happy for you. This family is really changing. I know your mother will be pleased. See if you can't bring Jane to Cove Valley to meet your mother."

"Well, I think the Knoxes and Mom know each other very well. They spent a lot of time together in the Indian villages."

"Yes, of course. How could I forget?" John shook his head with a rueful smile.

"John McClintock wants to come with us Martins. He seems to not be sure about having a family, And there is your Uncle Robert. He is back on the farm taking care of things. We will be fine. You do what you need to do. That piece of land that you bought in Cove Valley is good land."

Hugh was more than a little nervous about meeting with William Knox. He had never been involved the marriage thing before. This was a totally new experience, asking for the delightful girl's hand. It began to sink into him that this would be about the rest of their lives. He looked again for Jane. When their eyes met, he thought: this is the one I want to spend the rest of my life with and gladly so.

Later, he and William Knox were caring for the horses and Hugh told the older man that he wanted to marry Jane.

William Knox looked at Hugh as if he were demented.

"You want a woman who has been with the Indians?" he said harshly. "You don't look like you would be that desperate. If it is my land you are after, you can't think twice about it."

Hugh, thoroughly shocked, turned a fiery red. He took a deep breath and tried to control his anger.

"Perhaps I have not made myself very clear. I do not need your help to start a family. My prospects are very good. I have been working as a law clerk in Philadelphia. Jane and I would live there until I can buy a plantation of my own. I have seen a piece of land just ten miles from here. I have made an offer for it. I will be able to support a family either by raising the great horses or by doing legal work. As for the circumstances of your daughter, you, of all people, should know that God forgives and blesses us. It is unfortunate that some people would rather die than forgive. It is sad that some people cannot recognize their blessings. Some people can't seem to do anything but to hold tight to their hatreds."

Hugh did not back away or back down from the older man. He glared into Knox's eyes until Knox turned away.

William's shoulders sagged. "You are right, young man. I have been nursing my hatred of those savages. How could I take it out on my girl? Or on my wife? I just feel guilty that I could not protect them from harm. I should not have brought them into the wilderness."

"Well, they know the wilderness now as you and I never can. They seem pretty healthy to me. Let us put on big smiles and not have this conversation ever again."

"Young man, my girl is fortunate to have your attention. I think you will be a good provider for her." William took a deep, fresh breath, straightened his shoulders and shook Hugh's proffered hand.

Epilogue

General Jeffery Amherst   He was the one who recommended that the Indians be given blankets infected with small pox. That suggestion was not carried out by Col. Bouquet.

Amherst refused to take command of British forces when the revolution broke out. He felt that the rebels would win. After his return to England, he was given charge of the home forces by George III even though he was 75. He died at 79 in Kent in 1797.

Colonel John Armstrong   He went back to surveying after the war. He surveyed John Martin's property in 1769. Armstrong County, Pennsylvania bears his name, Kittanning is the county seat.

Henri Bouquet   In 1765, Bouquet was promoted to Brigadier General and placed in charge of all the king's forces in the southern colonies. He died in Pensacola, West Florida on September 2, 1765, perhaps from yellow fever.

Daniel Boone 1734-1820   In 1775 he blazed the Wilderness Road through the Cumberland Gap to Kentucky. Before 1800, 200,000 had entered Kentucky. He was a Militia officer from 1775-1783. He was captured and adopted by the Shawnees in 1778. He went into debt from land speculation (which was common with our heroes.) Moved to Missouri. Was a legend in his own time.

George Croghan   He was a great positive force on the frontier. After Pontiac's rebellion, he went to Detroit (Pontiac's home) to finalize a settlement with the Indians. While he was Wm. Johnson's *Deputy of Indian Affairs* he traveled constantly. Sometimes he was buying more land.

At the outset of the Revolution he was a charter member of the Ohio Company as were many famous men. He claimed 300,000 acres of land. During the Revolution, Croghan was accused of being a Tory and so lost all land claims. He died penniless in Philadelphia in 1782.

Governor Robert Dinwiddie of Virginia   He organized the first resistance to French incursions into the Ohio country. He retired to England. He died one month after his protégé, Robert Stobo.

The Marquis Duquesne   He was in charge of prisoners at Quebec when Stobo arrived there and permitted him much freedom. He rejoined the French Navy becoming a Vice-Admiral. He lost a naval battle to the British in 1758 and was taken prisoner and then paroled. Duquesne received a pension and retired to his estate outside Paris. He died in 1778 at the age of 78.

Francis Fauquier   He was Governor of Virginia until his death in 1768 at 64. Fauquier warned William Pitt that if the tax policies continued, the Colonies would resist. Fauquier dissolved the Virginia House of Burgesses in 1765 when it passed Patrick Henry's resolution against the Stamp Act. It was hoped that the Stamp Act would help pay for debts incurred during the French and Indian War.

La Force   He was the French officer who guided Washington and was captured at Jumonville Glen. He was returned to Montreal in 1760.

Captain Jack, the mythical   After an horrendous attack on an Indian camp at present day Saltsburg, Pennsylvania, he seemed to have appeased his rage and quit the Indian raids.

Elizabeth Knox   Lived long and died a spinster.

Robert Knox   He served as an officer in the Revolution. Owned land left to him by his father in Ligonier, Pennsylvania.

Susanna Knox   Sister to Robert and Jane. Married a lawyer named Robert Alexander and lived in Bedford, Pennsylvania.

Susan Knox   We lost track of William's heroic wife, mother of the four Knox children. We presume she lived long and died before William, in Ligonier.

William Knox   He lived long and left two large parcels of land in Ligonier to his four children, Jane, Robert, Susanna, and Elizabeth.

Hugh Martin   He was appointed magistrate in Westmoreland County Pennsylvania by the Colonial Council in 1769. He moved to the farm near Lycippus, Westmoreland County, Pennsylvania.

He was appointed Magistrate before the Revolution elected Magistrate after the Revolution. He was a Captain in the

Revolution. He married Jane Knox and they had nine children. Jane died in 1817 and Hugh died in 1823. His property had a church and a school. He was a devout Presbyterian. He is honored by a stone at Middle Presbyterian Church Cemetery, Mt. Pleasant, PA.

Charles Richard Martin   is a direct descendant through Hugh's eldest son, James, who married Huguenot Mary Leasure and moved to Darlington, Beaver County, Pennsylvania. James and Mary had nine children, one of whom was James Powers Martin who was Sheriff of Beaver County.

JP's son, William Hugh Martin, moved to Beaver Falls, ten miles from Darlington. W.H. was both realtor and Insurance agent. His son, James Wilmer Martin was an attorney and Assistant District attorney for Beaver County.

That brings us to the writer of this book, Charles Richard Martin, photographer, married co-writer Sara Mitchell and had Catherine, who also married a Mitchell, Gary. Her daughter is Caitlin Mitchell. William McQuaid Martin married Laurie Kassab. Their daughter is Elizabeth Martin. He also married Lisa Mitchell and they had Lauren Martin and Zachery Martin. Charles' third child is Thomas Alan Martin. He married Teresa Schnaubelt and they had Charles Thomas Jefferson Martin.

Janet Martin   The much traveled little Janet. She married John Jamison in Westmoreland County. Janet lived to be 83 at an area called Dry Ridge that had a rich vein of coal that brought prosperity to the Jamison family of Greensburg, Pennsylvania. She is the one who told the story of the Indian capture. She also told of having to keep fires going to keep wolves away when her husband John was not home.

James Martin   He and his brother William both moved to the land that had been an Indian camp, perhaps Chief Joseph's, where they were held for a time in captivity. It is believed that they are both buried in the Sewickley Presbyterian Cemetery on Sewickley Creek in Westmoreland County, grave sites 22 and 23.
   His brother Hugh lived at the headwaters of Sewickley Creek. James was a Captain in the Revolution. James was married.

John Martin   The hero of our story; he finally received title to his land in 1769. We believe that he and Margery rest in the Martin Cemetery on a farm near McConnellsburg, Fulton County, PA. The property had had a church and a school. He had 11 deeds to land over a period of time. Was he a land speculator? Most everyone else was.

Martha Martin   She married Hugh Bingham and lived within a mile of her brother Hugh Martin.

William Martin   He served in the Revolution as a lieutenant and is buried in the same Sewickley Presbyterian Cemetery at Bells Mills, PA as his brother, James.

Daniel Morgan 1735-1802   He was a pioneer, soldier, and US House of Rep. from Virginia. One of the most gifted battlefield tacticians of the Revolution. He was almost killed by a punishment of 500 lashes when just a 17 year old drover during Braddock's campaign. He so detested the arrogance of British officers toward the Colonial American forces during the French and Indian War that he later devised a special test to recruit sharpshooters for the Revolution: he had a large picture of a British officer, or perhaps it was King George, that the sharpshooter recruit was to target. If he hit the king with the first shot from his rifle at 100 yards, he was accepted into Morgan's sharpshooters. The battle in the movie **The Patriot** depicted General Morgan's tactics at the winning battle at Cowpens.

William Pitt   He who for whom Pittsburgh, Pennsylvania was named. He was Prime Minister of England. He spoke in favor of the colonies in their resistance to taxation but was not ready to grant them independence. When granted the status of "Earl," the "Great Commoner" lost much respect. He was recalled in 1766 to head the government again. In 1778 at the age of 70, he was addressing the House of Lords When he was seized by a convulsion. He was taken home and died shortly thereafter. He is buried in Westminster Abbey. He is featured in the movie "***Amazing Grace***" about the banning of slavery in the British Empire.

Shingas the Terrible   He was the brother of King Beaver. He terrorized the Pennsylvania, Maryland, and Virginia frontier from 1755-1758. He made peace with the English and was helpful in restoring peace to the area. It is written that he died in 1764, possibly at Muskingum.

The Beaver High School yearbook in Sara Mitchell Martin's hometown, Beaver, PA is called "The Shingas."

Lt. Simon Stevens He escaped with Robert Stobo from Quebec and also returned with him for the battle. After the war, Stevens lived in Springfield, Vermont, serving as Justice of the Peace for 50 years. During the Revolution he became a Captain, Major, and finally a Lt. Colonel. His career was remarkably similar to that of Hugh Martin.

Lt. Robert Stobo Stobo and Van Braam were made hostages after the Battle of Fort Necessity (Great Meadow). The two were to be exchanged later for Ens. LaForce and 20 French soldiers.

While a hostage at Quebec, Stobo tried to escape several times before being successful. In 1759, shortly before the Battle of Quebec, General Wolfe gave Stobo messages for General Amherst and Governor Pownell of Massachusetts, and so he missed the Battle of Quebec for which his information was so important. While on this mission, his ship was overtaken by a French privateer. Stobo weighted down the message packet and threw it overboard and then donned seaman's clothing to hide his identity. The French took everything of value and set the captives ashore near Halifax. Stobo made his way to Governor Pownell and eventually to Amherst where he gave an account of his mission.

Stobo went back to the Virginia Assembly who gave him 1000 pounds in addition to his back pay, an unheard of honor. He was granted some acreage in land Virginia claimed. Seeking another commission as an officer, he traveled back to England to plead for it.

Once again, in the English Channel, a French Privateer captured him. He had to pay a ransom of 125 pounds to go free.

He retrieved his hidden uniform which had in a pocket, a letter from General Monckton to William Pitt. Had he been found with this it would have been the death sentence (again).

William Pitt wrote to General Amherst suggesting he award Stobo a command. Amherst agreed. Under Amherst, Stobo aided in the taking of Montreal, ending the French rule in Canada.

In 1761, Major General Monckton was in charge of an expedition to the Caribbean for an assault on Martinique and Stobo was along. Afterwards they assaulted Spanish possessions including Cuba. The siege of Cuba went on and on and there was much sickness, and shortages of food and water. After 44 days Havana fell. During the battle, Spanish artillery hit a wall and caused it to fall on Stobo, fracturing his skull. Stobo went to New York with other wounded.

His life took a long downturn after the injury. In 1770, back in England, he made bad land investments. He got tangled in bureaucratic horrors and his head injury bothered him. His behavior was erratic. He drank too much. He took his own life with a pistol. He was only forty-three.

His oldest sister Janet Richardson, contrived a story that Stobo was on a ship going back to the colonies when a storm came up and all hands went down with the ship. George Washington made an offer to the Richardsons for the acreage in Virginia. It was not accepted.

Good enough story for a book? Try **The Extraordinary Adventures of Major Robert Stobo** by Robert C. Alberts.

Jacob VanBraam He was on the trip Washington made to Ft. Le Beouf and a hostage after the battle at Fort Necessity. After his release at Quebec, he was given a captain's commission in the Royal Americans Regiment.

After the Peace of Paris, in 1783, he was given half pay. He spent three years trying to get back in the army. At the outbreak of the Revolution, he was sent (on the British side) to St. Augustine, Florida with 150 recruits. He retired from the service in 1779 to his farm in Wales. The date and site of his death is unknown.

George Washington

After the disastrous battle at Ft. Necessity, Washington retired but not for long. He was at the side of Braddock, as an aide, through three hours of the battle, and helped carry the wounded general from the field.

Washington spent much time and money trying to establish his claims to 32,373 acres of land. He went to inspect the land in 1771 with George Croghan. The claim had been moved down the Ohio River to the Kanawha and Washington was not pleased. He wrote Stobo to tell him that his claim for 9000 acres had been granted. Stobo was dead. Washington had a tour of duty at Ft. Ligonier.

Washington died at Mt. Vernon in December 1799 at the age of 67. He had been busy. He was a leader in the Virginia opposition to the crown. And oh, yes. He commanded the Continental Armies. He was a delegate to the Constitutional Convention. He was first President of the United States of America.

In 1776, on the eve of the battle of New York that he would probably not win, Washington wrote that he recalled the humiliating loss at Great Meadows: "I did not let the anniversary of the 3rd (of July, 1753) pass off without a grateful remembrance of the escape we had.

The same Providence that protected us will, I hope, continue His mercies, and make us happy instruments in restoring peace and liberty." First in war. First in peace. First in the hearts of his countrymen.

Acknowledgements

Rock and Elaine Foster, The Beanery Writers and Carolyn Holland, Anita Hendrix,

Terry Schnaubelt Martin for the cover art work.

Scott Kubay for comments and editing.

Charles Martin for maps and photos.

Thanks to the wonderful, encouraging people in these libraries and historical places:

Baltzer-Meyer Library	Greensburg, PA
Beaver Falls Public Library	Beaver Falls, PA
Beaver Public Library	Beaver, PA
Bushy Run Battlefield	Harrison City, PA
DAR Library; Rick and Roz Ashmun	Mt. Pleasant, PA
Ft. Necessity Battle Field	Farmington, PA
Ft. Ligonier	Ligonier, PA
Fulton County Library	McConnellsburg, PA
Ligonier Valley Library; Pennsylvania Room; Shirley Iscrup:	Ligonier, PA
Little Beaver Historical Society	Darlington, PA
Meyersdale Library	Meyersdale, PA
Westmoreland Historical Society	Greensburg, PA